Frank Trollope

Captain Haverty's wooing

Vol. II

Frank Trollope

Captain Haverty's wooing
Vol. II

ISBN/EAN: 9783337043827

Printed in Europe, USA, Canada, Australia, Japan

Cover: Foto ©ninafisch / pixelio.de

More available books at www.hansebooks.com

CAPTAIN HAVERTY'S WOOING.

A Novel.

BY

FRANK TROLLOPE,

AUTHOR OF
'BROKEN FETTERS,' 'THE MARKED MAN,' 'AN OLD MAN'S SECRET,'
'A WOMAN'S ERROR,' ETC., ETC.

IN THREE VOLUMES.
VOL. II.

LONDON:
CHARLES J. SKEET, 10, KING WILLIAM STREET,
·CHARING CROSS.
1880.
[*All Rights Reserved.*]

CAPTAIN HAVERTY'S WOOING.

CHAPTER I.

CAPTAIN HAVERTY's mind became again unsettled after his unexpected meeting with the faithful attendant of Blanche Wyndham. He had endeavoured to force himself into a belief that it was better to yield to what seemed the inevitable lot of them both, and to force back into his own heart his blighted hopes and crushed affections, and to think that it would be better to avoid, as much as possible, everything that might tend to keep alive feelings and sentiments which, alas! had been already doomed to such early disappointment, than to make any further effort to renew the intercourse and tender regard which had so long subsisted between Blanche and himself, but which she had herself now broken off; believing that he was acting not only in accordance with her wishes in doing so, but also in a spirit most becoming his own character and personal honour, however much it might be contrary to the secret, affectionate clingings of his own heart, and the long-cherished hopes of his once anticipated happiness; but now these affections and hopes began to revive, and his settled purpose of yielding to his fate was considerably shaken.

For himself, nothing on earth would have made him change his resolution; but the thought that she, the bright, innocent playmate of his childhood, the gay-hearted gentle companion of his boyhood, and the beautiful, trusting object of his youthful love and admiration, the source of so much felicity and the subject of so many bright dreams of happiness to him in the midst of his long absence, struggles, and dangers; that she, who had thrown her gentle arms round his neck and sobbed upon his breast in all the intensity of long-cherished, unacknowledged love, and all the agony of parting affection, when he left her to go forth to fight for his country; that she was about to be for ever torn from him, and to become the wife of one not only so utterly unworthy of her, but for whom she evidently had the very greatest aversion and dislike, instead of confidence and love, and from whom she had so little prospect of future respect, regard, or happiness—that this was the impending fate of Blanche Wyndham, and that it might possibly be in his power to avert it! But that he should stand aloof, and not make one effort to do so, when she perhaps, too, looked for his help, was more than he could think of or contemplate without both anxiety and emotion.

Every day he seemed, by some strange accident or other, to become more and more acquainted with not only the worthlessness and baseness of Mr. James Murray's character, but with the absolute rottenness of his position, as well as his utter disregard for her about to be sacrificed by the infatuated blindness of her parents to his unprincipled scheme of falsehood and deception. Ought he not, therefore, to advise them for their own sakes, and for their daughter's future happiness, to make some inquiries into the statements and assertions that Mr. Murray had doubtless made respecting his position, and by which they had been deceived into a belief of the suitableness of the alliance, before the fatal project was complete.

This was a question that he found it very difficult to answer. In the first place his sense of honour made him shrink from repeating what he had accidentally heard, knowing that it was not intended for his ear, and felt as if, in doing so, it would be almost like a betrayal of confidence on his part; and in the second place, even if he did, would they believe him?

Again and again thoughts passed through his mind, and again and again was he withheld from acting upon them by these considerations. Still he felt far from satisfied in his own heart, and would gladly now, at all events, have taken advantage of any circumstances that might have given him a fair excuse for once more seeing Blanche Wyndham and ascertaining from her own lips how far any efforts on his part to interpose between her and her impending union with Mr. James Murray would meet her approval, and be in accordance with her own secret hopes and wishes.

But after the painful emotions excited in her by his last visit, he could scarcely, under any circumstances, muster sufficient resolution to call again at her father's house ; and after the letter that he had received from her, he felt it would be almost rudeness for him to seek any interview with her. And might not the servant, after all, be mistaken in her opinions of the feelings of her young mistress, and fancy that her mind was dwelling upon him, when probably he was the last person she cared to think about?

It might be so. Still something within him seemed to tell him it was not so. There was a small, still voice whispering to his heart, that he alone possessed the power of making Blanche Wyndham happy, as she alone could make him so ; and that he ought not to yield her up and consign her to a life of wretchedness with another, or to a broken heart or an early grave, without making one more effort to save her from so fearful a fate, although how he was to do so he could not tell.

With these thoughts passing through his mind, and without having arrived at any satisfactory conclusion with himself, William Haverty strolled on towards his father's house, taking a slightly circuitous path to avoid going close past Bilford Hall, in case of meeting any of the Wyndhams, or being seen by their servants.

Just as he was approaching the gate that led from the road to his father's house, he was not a little surprised to see Mr. and Mrs. Ingram driven out in their carriage, and turn off in the opposite direction, probably to make a call at their son's, a little further on.

How to account for this unexpected visit was beyond his power. Could it be about anything on the part of Mr. James Murray, to try and ascertain from them if they had any suspicion of that gentleman's real position? Or could it have arisen out of his own brief interview with Mr. Ingram at the bank, and his taking out the full remittance instead of leaving it there to be drawn as occasion required? Or could that gentleman have taken offence at his doing so, and himself brought his father's money, and closed his account with the bank? It might be so, but he could scarcely think it. Or, might it not be—as he had seen them call at the Wyndhams'— that they had brought some message from them to his father and mother, or possibly to himself? Or, perhaps Blanche was dangerously ill; and they had called to inform them of it!"

With this fear spurring him on, he hurriedly walked up to the door to learn the cause of this unexpected visit from the two important personages who had just left the house.

'Who do you think, William, we have just had a visit from?' exclaimed the colonel, as his son entered.

'The Ingrams,' replied the son. 'I saw their carriage going out at the gate as I approached it.'

'You didn't know they were coming, did you?' inquired his father. 'Mr. Ingram said he had seen you at the bank, and I thought he seemed rather disappointed at not meeting you, as he said he was in hopes you would have got home before they arrived here.'

'Why, he must have known I hadn't got home. They passed me twice on the road, as I was coming."

'Indeed! He didn't say anything about that. Perhaps he did not observe you.'

'Oh yes, he did; though neither of them pretended to notice me. I came round by the lanes, passed General Fielden's house, where they dashed by me, and in at his gate, just as I was passing it; and again in the narrow lane between that and Bilford Hall, where they also called, as I saw their carriage being driven up to the house from the height where I was. I suppose they did not find the general at home, as they were only a few minutes in passing me again.'

'I don't expect they did, as he called here about an hour, or an hour and a half ago, and had not been very long gone when they came in. They didn't say anything of having called either upon him or the Wyndhams. You didn't meet General Fielden on the road, I suppose; he was on horseback.'

'No, I turned a little to the right instead of coming down by Bilford Hall, and came round by the footpath across the hillside. The Ingrams didn't remain long here, or I should have seen them.'

'No. They wanted to call on their son, they said, as they were so near; and were anxious to get back soon, as they were going out after they got home, to dine at Sir William Gosport's.'

'Well, how did you like Mrs. Ingram, mother?' inquired her son, as she entered the room.

'Oh, only middling. She assumes rather too many airs, and affects rather too much grandeur for me, William; some of which don't seem to sit very easily upon her,' replied Mrs. Haverty, quietly.

'Well, I scarcely expected you would, although you have met her before,' remarked the son.

'Yes, but I don't think I ever spoke half-a dozen words to her at any time. Besides, as we have been so many years here, and she has never before done us the honour of calling, it was hardly worth the while doing so now.'

'I thought it rather odd, too,' said the colonel; 'and though I have seen Mr. Ingram often, both at his bank and other places, I confess I have never felt any great inclination for increasing my acquaintance with him. There is a kind of silly pomposity about him that I think is very foolish, especially in so old a man.'

'I don't think his wife is much better in that respect,' said William.

'Indeed she is not, William,' returned his mother. 'I've no patience with such absurd affectation in an old woman.'

'Well, she must have been very bad to have put you out of patience, mother,' rejoined her son, with a smile. 'Did Mr. Ingram tell you that I had drawn the whole of my remittance?' he inquired, addressing his father.

'Yes ; and I had some idea at first, when he mentioned it, that he was not over-well pleased about it, as if he thought you were afraid to trust the money in his bank.'

'I don't see why he should have been at all displeased about that, unless he felt that there was real cause for my being afraid to let it remain in his bank,' returned the son.

'But you don't mean to say that you are, William?' said the colonel, with an incredulous smile. 'You did not think that your five hundred pounds was going to make them abscond to Australia, did you? Why, they have had more than four times that sum of mine in their hands for the last dozen years, and I never dreamed of such a catastrophe. Mr. Wyndham, too, has always a large amount in their bank, and so has General Fielden : and I don't think it ever entered into their heads that there was any danger in its being there.'

'I don't say that there is, only I overheard something to-day which rather shook my confidence in the enormous wealth of Messrs. Ingram and Day.'

'Indeed!' said his father, with a rather uneasy look. 'But it must be a mistake. The very thing that made me imagine Mr.

Ingram was not over-pleased at your drawing out the whole of your money, was his saying that just now they had so much money in their hands that they could hardly find employment for it, and asking me if I didn't think I could find some other investment for what I have deposited there, as, money being so plentiful, they found paying me four per cent. for it was as much, if not more, than they could get themselves; though I have not drawn the interest for the last year or two.'

'Well, that's rather strange,' replied William, with a puzzled look, and hardly agrees with what I heard from Mr. Ingram's own lips this morning,' he added, proceeding to give his father an account of the conversation he had overheard between Mr. Ingram and Mr. Murray in the bank.

'Humph! As far as regards Murray, it looks very bad. It is very plain that he, at all events, is in a state of absolute ruin, and is trying to repair his broken fortunes by marrying Blanche Wyndham. This is a most abominable thing, when it is evident he does not care a straw for herself, and that she also as strongly objects to him; but that his sole object in deceiving her parents, with his assumed position and wealth, is to get hold of their daughter for the sake of their property. It was, perhaps, the knowledge of his position that induced Mr. Ingram to speak as he did, and to seem rather unwilling to advance him the money; for it is plain enough he is only going to let him have it in hopes of being able to recover some of his other advances afterward, or for some other purpose of his own. But it is a most disgraceful thing for Mr. Ingram to countenance and assist in such a scheme of villany and deception against the happiness of Blanche Wyndham and her parents, and to involve them in his ruin; but they ought to be made acquainted with it.'

'It is most infamous, I think,' said Mrs. Haverty, warmly, 'that poor Blanche should be made the victim of such a heartless scheme, and that her parents should have become so blinded and deceived by that man Murray; and those Ingrams are just as bad for helping him.'

'Quite, my dear,' replied her husband, earnestly; 'and if I had known this when they were here, I should have taken Ingram at his word, and drawn out my money, and had nothing more to do with either him or his bank.'

'Well, I think I should do so yet, father,' rejoined the son. 'The very fact of his calling here to-day, after what I overheard, and his never having done so before, makes me feel all the more convinced that the opinion I have formed of Messrs. Ingram and Day's Bank is correct. It looks to me very much as if he had merely done this to throw you off your guard, or to dispel any suspicions that my drawing out the money made him, perhaps, fancy you had; not so much for the sake of what you have in the bank yourself, as from the effect your doubts on the subject might have with General Fielden, who I should suppose has a very large sum in their hands.'

'Well, it looks very like it. In fact, I feel quite sure it is the case,' returned the colonel; 'for I know General Fielden, a year or two ago, drew a very large sum indeed, somewhere about twenty thousand pounds, I believe, out of the Funds, and placed it in the bank, by the advice of Mr. Ingram, who took it as if he was doing so only as a favour to the colonel, to give him better interest for it.'

'The more I think of it, the more suspicious it looks,' resumed the son.

'So it does to me, William,' rejoined the colonel, thoughtfully and uneasily. 'I don't like the look of it, and almost wish I had taken Mr. Ingram at his word.'

'You ought to do it at once, I think. I may certainly be mistaken in my opinion; but even if I am, it will only be erring on the safe side; and if the Ingrams should be offended, we have no occasion to mind that.'

'Offended! Why, after the way they are assisting that scoundrel Murray in his abominable scheme of deception and cruelty to Blanche Wyndham, that is about the last consideration I should care for,' exclaimed the colonel, indignantly. 'I only wish I had not promised to let the money remain in their hands; otherwise I shouldn't have troubled myself upon that score. But he told me, when I said I had no need of the money at present, and didn't wish to draw it out of his bank, that if I really wished it to remain, he had no objection to it; only as he must look out for some means of employing it profitably, I must not expect him to keep it at my command in the bank, but that he should require at least six or nine months' notice if I should wish to withdraw it, which I agreed to.'

'Oh, indeed!' said William, with much

more uneasiness than he wished to show. 'But do you consider you bound yourself in any way to abide by that promise? If you were to let him know at once that you have changed your mind and wished the money, I don't see that it can interfere with any investment he is going to make, as he has not had time yet to do anything with it. But of course you know best.'

'Well, I hardly know what to do. You see, I told him I didn't require the money, and agreed to his proposal about the six or nine months' notice before withdrawing it. So, after that, I fear I can hardly tell him I want it.'

'But an understanding of that kind is not binding on you, especially as you have only now verbally made it,' rejoined the son.

'Perhaps not legally, William; but morally it is, as well as socially. After having promised, I cannot break my word.'

'No; if you look at it in that light, I don't say that you can. Only a business sort of thing like this, that involves nothing but simply a change of opinion, scarcely seems to me to deserve being regarded in so important a light.

'Perhaps not, William. Still, I do not feel

in my own mind as if I should be acting honourably in withdrawing the money now,' returned the colonel. 'What do you say, my dear?' he inquired, appealing to his wife.

'Well, my dear,' replied Mrs. Haverty, with affectionate confidence, 'I confess I am very anxious about the money, and wish you had not promised to let that cunning man have it any longer; but about your withdrawing it now I dare not attempt to give any advice. The safety of so large a sum of money is a very important thing for both us and our dear children; but your honour is the first thing to be considered, for that is far more to me, and to them too, than the money.'

'Thank you, my old darling! I know you always look to that first, and prize it above every other consideration.'

So it was resolved that the money should remain in the hands of Messrs. Ingram and Day, as promised by the major to Mr. Ingram. In the sensitiveness of his honour, the gallant old soldier determined rather to risk his money than break his word, though, under the circumstances, in a merely business point of view, which was the only one that most people would have looked at it, there was nothing either binding upon him or reprehensible if he had decided otherwise; nor did either his wife or his son attempt to alter his determination, for they were not less sensitive upon the subject of his honour than the colonel was himself, and had too much confidence in his judgment and regard for his affection either to doubt his anxiety to preserve his property from risk, or to murmur at his even imperilling that, rather than endanger his honour. This, however, did not prevent them from resolving to communicate their fears as to the safety of the bank to General Fielden, and advising him that he might take some means either to ascertain how far their suspicions were well-founded, or to secure his money, if possible, before it was too late, even though his doing so should involve the loss of their own, which the colonel felt he could not honourably withdraw after what had just passed between himself and Mr. Ingram.

'Oh! by-the-bye,' said the colonel, after a short pause, 'talking about those Ingrams and their bank has almost made me forget to tell you about the general's call and his message for you. He's going to have his usual Christmas-eve party on Friday, and has asked us all to go and dine with him. Your mother and I tried to get off, as we haven't been at anything of the kind during your absence, and we are getting too old to care about going out; but he would not let us off, and insisted upon our going, if it were only in honour of your safe return home. So we consented to accompany you if you went; and he desired us to give you his very kind regards, and to say that he fully counts upon your going, and won't take a refusal.'

'Well, I am hardly in spirits—I mean I am hardly in the humour or health to go out to any parties at present,' replied William, half hesitatingly.

'We told him that we were afraid you might not be able to go on that account, but he declared he would not hear of any such excuse,' said the colonel, smiling.

'Well, I don't know. I would much rather not go, and if it had been an invitation from anyone else, I should have declined without a moment's hesitation.'

'So should we,' replied the colonel; 'but he urged it so strongly and seemed so unwilling to accept a refusal, that we were at last forced to give a half-reluctant consent, provided you were inclined to go, and thought it would not hurt you.'

' Ah, well! I don't apprehend that it would do me any harm, only I don't feel as if I cared about going out anywhere at present. Are there to be many there, do you know?'

'I daresay there will be a good many. But he said you needn't fear meeting anyone that you didn't like; which, I suppose, means that he's not going to ask Mr. James Murray.'

'Well, I suppose that worthy would be just as unwilling to meet me as I should be to meet him. But I suppose those Ingrams will be there, and I daresay the Days, none of whom I am at all solicitous about meeting again.'

' Yes, they are sure to be there; and after what you heard passing between Mr. Ingram and Mr. Murray to-day, and the suspicions we have about their bank, it will be rather awkward meeting them there—especially if you tell General Fielden, as you propose doing—and I fully think it ought to be done,' returned the colonel.

' If I tell him at all, I think I ought to do so at once; and yet perhaps it would make it disagreeable if I did so before his party; and then again, I hardly know how to tell him. It seems such a mean thing to listen to what other people are saying, even though one has not done so intentionally, and to tell what one hears in that way afterwards,' said William, half musingly.

'Yes, but under the circumstances in which you heard it, and the singular manner in which you have become acquainted with the very important matter you have to communicate, he will never for a moment either judge unfavourably of your character or misconstrue your motives in telling him, even if he should not act upon your information,' returned the colonel. 'But perhaps it may be as well to wait till after the party, especially if we are likely to go to it. He told us that little Miss Day would be there with her father and mother.'

'I care just as little for seeing them as I do the Ingrams.'

'They are no great favourites of mine, either,' remarked Mrs. Haverty, quietly. 'They are too much like their friends the Ingrams.'

'I'm afraid you don't appreciate the high honour the Ingrams have just conferred upon us, or their important position in the neighbourhood, my dear,' said the colonel, good-humouredly.

'Indeed I do not, if appreciation means being flattered with it.'

'I suppose we must go. What do you say, mother?' inquired William.

'Yes, I think we must. General Fielden is such an old friend, and is such an excellent kind-hearted man, that I should not like to hurt his feelings by staying away; for I am quite sure he would feel it, if we did not go.'

'Very well then, as far as I am concerned I am quite willing to accept his invitation,' replied William. 'I suppose we must send a note to tell him we shall come?'

'Or you can walk along and tell him yourself,' rejoined the colonel.

CHAPTER II.

For two years, neither Colonel nor Mrs. Haverty had attended General Fielden's Christmas-eve party. The absence of their son, and the knowledge of the privations and dangers he was undergoing in the Crimea, created too great a blank in their hearts, and too much anxiety in their minds, to allow them to have any pleasure in such scenes of social enjoyment; but now that he had returned home, and the strong contrast no longer presented itself to their thoughts, of the difference between the safety and luxuries they possessed, with his absolute want of common comforts, altered the case.

The gallant old colonel especially felt this. His natural flow of high spirits and lively temper, which had often been greatly depressed and saddened at the thought of not only his son's fearful sufferings, but those of the whole army, and often, too, not a little inflamed with indignation at the culpable mismanagement and want of foresight of the government, who had first allowed the country, by their utter want of manly activity, to be drawn into a war which would never have occurred but for their known incapability of directing the energies of the nation.

But now that his gallant son had been preserved amid it all, and was returned home to gladden the hearts of himself and his affectionate wife, he was willing to forget, as far as he could, both his own anxieties on his son's account and his rancour against the unfortunate men who had been at the head of affairs when the mismanagement occurred, and was ready to give vent to the long-pent-up natural gaiety of his heart, and cheerfulness of his spirits, in more general intercourse with his friends and neighbours than he had done of late.

For several years past Mrs. Haverty, when present at any of General Fielden's parties, had always acted as hostess, by taking the head of the dinner-table, or presiding at the tea-table, and on this occasion she was to resume her wonted position.

The general received his old friends and their son with great courtesy and the sincerest pleasure. He had asked them to come early, that Mrs. Haverty might be ready to assist him in the reception of his other guests.

'I am sorry to say our old friends the Wyndhams are not able to join us this time,' he said, addressing Mrs. Haverty; while William, though he scarcely expected to have met Blanche there, felt a chilling sense of disappointment creep over his heart as he was thus assured of it. 'I have called at their house twice, to see if I could prevail upon them to come; but they do not seem in spirits, and I understand their daughter is very poorly. I have not even seen her when I have called there lately.'

'Indeed! I am very sorry to hear it,' replied Mrs. Haverty. 'Poor Blanche! I am afraid she does not like this marriage that her father and mother have resolved upon, between herself and Mr. James Murray.'

'I am afraid so, too, and I'm very sorry to see them so determined to sacrifice the happiness of their daughter, in their anxiety to secure her a good position in society,' replied the general.

'I only hope they may not be mistaken in their views on this point,' rejoined Mrs. Haverty, quietly.

'Well, I have heard some whispers upon that, too; though I have always looked upon Mr. Murray as a man of large property, and he has a fine estate, you know. But I suppose the old people have taken care to ascertain all about that.'

'I should think so. And yet I have my doubts.'

'Indeed!' said the general; 'you surprise me! I confess I do not like the man very much. I believe he is a mean-spirited, bad man in many respects, and for this reason did not ask him to come here to-day. And perhaps that is the reason why the Wyndhams would not come; but I could not help it. I was so utterly disgusted with his conduct in that affair the other day with your son, or rather with your son's servant, that, even when I meet him on the bench, it is almost as much as I can do to be courteous to him; and I am deeply grieved that Miss Wyndham, who was always a great favourite of mine, is destined to become the wife of one so utterly unworthy of her as I believe him to be. Though in a social point of view I never imagined there was any reason to apprehend disappointment. In fact, I thought this was the only recommendation it had.'

'So did we till lately; but now, I fear, there is no less ground for uneasiness about that than the other,' returned Mrs. Haverty.

'What does your wife mean, colonel?' inquired the general, turning to her husband, who was standing with his son, looking out of the window upon the distant city, covering the sloping side of the elevated ground rising from the opposite side of the river.

'Why, I believe that this same Mr. James Murray, of Glemham Hall, is not only a cowardly humbug, as we know him to be, but a pretender and cheat into the bargain!' exclaimed the colonel, who never failed in giving hearty expression to his feelings and thoughts, whatever they might be.

'Well, that's strong enough, at all events: but do you really mean to say that you have reason to believe Mr. Murray not to be the man of property he is supposed to be, and ostensibly is?'

'Yes, I do; and I've a strong suspicion

that some other people we know, who are the chief aiders of this Mr. Murray in this heartless deception of the Wyndhams, are not much better either in principle or property,' replied the colonel, mysteriously. ' But, never mind,' he added after a moment's pause, assuming his accustomed tone and manner of lively gaiety ; ' we will not talk about this now. We shall have the rest of your guests here directly, Come and have lunch with us to-morrow, or in a few days, and we will tell you all about it, as perhaps the subject may be more interesting to you than you now suppose.'

' Very well, I will,' said the general, checking his curiosity, and little imagining how much he was concerned himself in the matter. ' And now, William,' he added, addressing our hero in a tone of friendly good-humour, ' there is a young lady coming whom I once fancied you admired a little, and who, I have a strong suspicion, is not blind to either your merits or your good looks.'

' Indeed,' said William, with a slightly confused smile, thinking rather of Blanche Wyndham than much interested as to who the young lady might be.

' Are you not curious to know who it is ?'

asked the host, with a half-bantering air. 'You look as if you didn't care a fig, for all the trouble I have taken to bring you together. Just like the thanks philanthropic people generally get for their endeavours to serve and benefit their fellow-creatures!'

'Oh, I assure you I feel very grateful to you indeed,' replied William, laughing ; 'and I hope, when I know who the young lady is, I shall fully appreciate your kindness. I hope she is young and pretty.'

'Well, she is young, and passably good-looking ; and, I suppose, will have a goodish fortune, if that's any recommendation.'

'Most decidedly it is, if her other qualities and attractions are in proportion, not otherwise.'

'You must judge for yourself. It is Miss Julia Day.'

'What!' said William, not at all disappointed, for he really felt very indifferent upon the subject, though the gaiety of youth and his good sense prevented him from becoming gloomy and misanthropic, and the natural gallantry of his spirits made him always feel a certain degree of interest and pleasure in the society of ladies. 'What!' he repeated, ' my little friend Julia Day ?'

'Yes; are you not much obliged to me now?'

'Of course I am: and I hope she is also.'

'Oh, I'm not afraid of her being ungrateful, if you're not.'

'Why, I thought that young lady was to have been married some time ago, general,' remarked Mrs. Haverty.

'So she was, I believe; at least she, as well as her mother, expected it. But you know how uncertain things are, Mrs. Haverty,' said he with a smile.

'Why, to my certain knowledge she has expected, or at all events tried hard, with the assistance of her mother, to be married two or three times.'

'Come, come! I won't allow you to traduce the character of so charming a young lady,' said General Fielden, good-humouredly, 'nor her mother either, who I think is very right to do what she can to secure a husband for her daughter. You had better take care they don't secure you, and then I shall tell them afterwards what you've said; for I've determined that you shall lead the young lady in to dinner.'

'Thank you, general; and if I don't behave myself properly, and treat her with all the respect and attention she deserves, hold a court-martial upon my conduct, and condemn me to everlasting celibacy and your displeasure,' said William, gaily; for he felt, and knew too well, what constituted the character of a gentleman not to know that courteous attention and politeness to ladies are always two of its most prominent features. Besides, every young man, unless his feelings have become morbidly blunted by disappointment unduly indulged, or his mind diseased by unhealthy sentimentality, feels a certain amount of pleasure and enjoyment in the intercourse and society of the opposite sex; and however slight may be the impression that they make upon the heart, there is always a degree of agreeable excitement at the time, which is both innocent and pleasant to indulge in.

In a few minutes the guests began to arrive, and were received by General Fielden in the drawing-room, with all the politeness and courtesy of good breeding, and a warm, generous heart.

Among the first who made their appearance were the Rev. John Anstruther and his pleasant little wife, and their eldest daughter, a tall, fresh-coloured, ladylike girl about nineteen. In spite of occasional differences of opinion upon theological questions, the worthy rector and Colonel Haverty entertained the highest esteem for each other, and always met with much pleasure and cordial good feeling; while Mrs. Haverty met his wife and daughter—for they were especial favourites with that good lady—and was delighted to see them, and have a little friendly gossip together.

Our hero, too, did not show any symptoms of being dissatisfied with the society of Jane Anstruther, for whom he had always entertained the greatest respect and esteem, but entered into conversation with her with the ease of a gentleman and the confidence of an old friend. Of course he received the hearty congratulations of both the rector and his wife, and their daughter also, on his return home, as well as on the honours and advancement he had won in the war; and a good-humoured rebuke from Mrs. Anstruther for not having called to see them since his return.

Shortly after the Anstruthers, the retired county court judge, Mr. Grant, and his wife arrived, who, after being welcomed by their gallant host, shook hands with the colonel and Mrs. Haverty, congratulated their son, and then joined the rector and his wife, the former of whom was rather a favourite with Mrs. Grant, on account of a certain community of theological views between them, combined with a certain kind of cheap philanthropy professed by that lady, with which she imposed upon the good-natured clergyman, and led him to consult her in various matters connected with the schools and poor of his parish. The judge himself was a small, lively, pleasant sort of man, who cared little about the theological opinions held by others, provided they did not interfere with his own, or the receipt of his salary or pension. But his wife was a lady of large proportions, extensive dress, lofty ideas as to her own importance in the county, and great pretensions as to extreme gentility and exclusive society, and adopted those views and doctrines of religious questions—without any reference whatever to either their merits or demerits, of which she was by no means qualified to judge—that she deemed most in accordance with the tastes and opinions of the fashionable circles in which she moved, and which were held by all the great dignitaries of the cathedral close by.

Several other guests quickly arrived, amongst whom were no less a personage than an archdeacon, belonging to the Westdon Cathedral, and his wife; very high and mighty people in their way, and great friends and allies of Mrs. Grant, especially in her ecclesiastical predilections and economical patronage of the poor.

Then came Mr. Ingram, junior, and his wife; the former, of course, in the full uneasiness of fashionable tailorship, and the latter in the quiet, half-timid composure of youthful maternity, amiability of disposition and ill-rewarded affection for the shallow puppy whom she had unfortunately allowed herself to be argued into marrying four or five years before, while she was yet in the unsuspicious youth of inexperienced girlhood and ignorance of the contemptible worthlessness of her pretended admirer. Both Colonel Haverty and his wife had great esteem for this gentle little creature, and often forced themselves to treat her husband with an appearance of respect they were far from feeling, out of regard for her. They therefore met her with much sincere good feeling; nor did their son fail to pay respectful deference to her well-known goodness and modest gentleness of demeanour;

feeling, too, much inward sympathy for the unfortunate lot by which she had become united to a man so utterly unworthy of her, and of whose faults she alone seemed to be ignorant, or, at least, looked as if she were, and strived to hide from the world.

Brave, good, noble-hearted woman! Go on in thy work, and may Heaven sustain thee in it and give thee thy reward!

But more important personages wait our notice. See, here comes Mr. and Mrs. Day: the former a plain, rather common-looking, short, stoutish, elderly man; and the latter a little, erect, haughty-looking, over-dressed woman, about the same age as her husband, though evidently not only trying to look much younger than she was, but really believing she did do so—and if the free use of cosmetics and rouge, false hair and artificial teeth, and juvenility of dress and affected simplicity of youthful manner, could have succeeded in making her look young, her efforts would have been most satisfactory. But alas! in spite of all these—in spite of her violent struggles with nature, and her incessant war against grey hairs, wrinkles, stiffening limbs, and other constituent attendants of advancing years, Mrs. Day could neither ward off the steady encroachments for herself, nor altogether conceal their effects from others.

Close behind Mr. and Mrs. Day followed Miss Julia Day, who was the youngest of three daughters, besides two or three sons. One of her elder sisters being rather an invalid, and the other married, she was the only one who now went regularly into society with her mother, with whom she had always been the favourite; probably because Mrs. Day saw reflected in her much of her own character, and that she was the youngest— thereby, she thought, lessening the probability of calling forth allusions respecting her own age.

Miss Julia Day was in her twenty-sixth year, but looked much younger. In fact, she had, at first sight especially, a girlish look about her round, rather pale face, and small, half-crafty-looking blue eyes, that gave her more the appearance of a girl in her teens than a young lady who had passed ha f through her third decade. Like both her parents, she was rather short; and, like her father, she was rather stout, which properties were still increased by great amplitude of crinoline and white skirts, low dress upon her soft, fat arms and shoulders, and a blue sash round her substantial waist. And yet the effect of the whole was rather amusing than disagreeable. Nor was her manner, though a good deal affected, by any means unpleasant. She was just the sort of little, self-important, half-designing coquette that a man sometimes likes to meet at a party, for the sake of the amusement he finds in her society, and the trifling kind of flirtation that may be carried on without any serious thoughts of ulterior consequences, or the fear of exciting sentiments that might disturb her mind afterward.

William Haverty was, therefore, not sorry at the prospect of finding relief from his own secret thoughts, and sad recollections of Blanche Wyndham, by a little harmless trifling with Miss Julia Day, whose character he knew too well to be under any anxiety about the effect it might have upon her feelings; although he knew well also that she was a most determined little flirt and schemer, and was plying every art to catch not only a permanent beau but a husband, in which laudable endeavour she was perseveringly assisted by her indulgently complacent, diplomatic mother.

'How do you do, Mr. William Haverty?' said the elegant little Mrs. Day, as she shook hands in a most friendly manner with him, after she had received the general's welcome, and shaken hands with the colonel and Mrs. Haverty. 'I'm so glad to see you safe home again after all your dangers, and to congratulate you on your honours, which, I assure you, have given us all at Sunnyside the greatest pleasure.'

'Thank you; I am most gratified to know of your good feelings and interest in me,' replied Captain Haverty, with a courteous smile. 'How do you do, Miss Day?' he added, extending his hand to that young lady, who stood with a feigned, half-bashful look beside her mother.

'Pretty well, thank you,' she replied, in a slightly affected tone of half-pleased confusion.

'I assure you, it is quite an unexpected pleasure to both my daughter and myself to meet you here,' remarked Mrs. Day, in her own juvenile, agreeable way. 'When did you return?'

'Oh, I have been home a week now,' replied the captain, who had his own doubts about their not having heard of it. He gave

Mrs. Day too much credit for knowing what was going on in the neighbourhood for that.

'Indeed? And you've never found time to call at Sunnydown House and see us! And such old friends as we are, too! That's too bad of you!' exclaimed Mrs. Day, in a tone of good-humoured reproof. 'And we all so anxious to see you.'

Captain Haverty had not been at Sunnydown House more than three or four times in his life, and had certainly never considered himself to be regarded there as strictly upon their visiting-list; he was, therefore, almost surprised to hear that Mrs. Day thought he should have called upon them; at the same time he felt, to a certain degree, gratified with the apparent courtesy of that lady. Without, therefore, acknowledging that he had not intended calling at all, he excused himself for not having done so by saying he had not had time or opportunity to commence his visits yet to his friends, owing to other matters which had occupied his time since his return home.

'Well, when you can find time, I hope you will call and see us. We shall be so delighted,' returned Mrs. Day warmly, with a glance at her daughter.

'Yes, we shall indeed,' added the young lady, who evidently understood her mother's look as a signal for her to make herself agreeable to him.

'You are very kind,' said he, 'and I hope I shall soon be able to have the pleasure of calling upon you.'

William Haverty strongly suspected that Mrs. Day was either not real—in fact he knew that there was very little that was real about her—but he suspected she was either not sincere in her pretended interest in him, or that she had some other object in view than simply respect for himself, in the extreme politeness and consideration she seemed all at once inclined to show him. He, however, replied to her friendly expressions with perfect courtesy, and betrayed no appearance of doubting the sincerity of her language or feelings.

'I believe I am to have the honour—that is to say if it is agreeable to you—General Fielden has promised me the pleasure of leading you in to dinner, Miss Day,' said our hero, addressing that young lady, who tried to look a little surprised, and gave a glance of feigned confusion at her mother, who immediately replied for her :

'Oh, Julia will be most happy, I know. She has always been an admirer of yours, you know,' she said, in a half-joking tone.

'Oh, ma! How can you?' said the young lady, with the prettiest little start imaginable, slightly colouring.

'Well, my child, you know I am only joking,' replied the mother, with a forced laugh. 'Captain Haverty is an old friend, and of course doesn't mind what I say.'

'Oh, but it is too bad, Mrs. Day, first to give me such an agreeable piece of intelligence, and then to say that I must not mind what you say,' rejoined William Haverty, with an air of well-feigned disappointment.

Just at this moment the entrance of Mr. and Mrs. Ingram caused a little stir in the room, and gave our hero an opportunity of turning round and speaking to one or two other people that he knew.

Without recognising or appearing to notice anyone else, the Ingrams, arm-in-arm, walked up to the host, who happened at that moment to be in conversation with Colonel Haverty and the archdeacon, at the opposite end of the room, and with an air of the most dignified courtesy received the cordial welcome of the gallant general; after which they shook hands with the archdeacon in a very friendly manner, for they belonged to the same set, and also with the colonel, for it suited Mr. Ingram's purpose, at present, to be courteous to him : and then the lady, whose dress and jewels were almost as magnificent as the air with which she wore them, swept across the room to the archdeacon's wife, who immediately made room for her on the couch on which she was sitting, and received her with an expression of the most friendly interest and satisfaction. At the same time Mrs. Ingram gave a half-formal, half-friendly bend of the head to Mrs. Day, whom she did not appear to have observed, and then each drew herself up with something of a jealous look in their cold, haughty countenances, for there was no small degree of secret rivalry between the wives of the two partners.

CHAPTER III.

A FEW minutes after the arrival of the Ingrams the butler entered and announced dinner, on which the host requested the gentlemen to lead their partners to the dining-room.

'As you are to be the hostess, I cannot do myself the honour of leading you in myself,' said the general in a half undertone to Mrs. Haverty, 'but I shall confer that distinction on the archdeacon,' beckoning that gentleman as he spoke, to the evident disappointment of one or two of the other ladies who had been angling for the honour.

'Here, archdeacon,' said he, 'you shall have the privilege of leading Mrs. Haverty to the head of the table.'

'Thank you, general,' he replied with wellbred courtesy, though perhaps with a little bit of loftiness in it, at the same time politely offering his arm to the lady. 'You do me great honour by allowing me the pleasure,' he added, as he led the way with Mrs. Haverty.

The colonel, who, on account of the assistance he required from her, always sat next his wife at table, followed with Mrs. James Ingram, who had been assigned to him by General Fielden, and for whose quiet manner and gentle goodness he had very great respect and regard. Then followed Mr. Anstruther with Mrs. Ingram, who seemed rather disappointed at being compelled to content herself with a clergyman who was only the rector of a small country parish, when there was an archdeacon in the room. Giving way to his wife and her partner, Mr. Ingram followed with Mrs. Grant, stalking and bowing to his partner with the grandeur of a man who knew his own importance, and the air of an old beau, which character he still retained. Then Mr. Grant with Mrs. Day, Mr. Day with Mrs. Anstruther, William Haverty with Miss Julia Day, and Mr. James Ingram with Miss Anstruther, rather to the annoyance of that young lady, who did not happen to entertain a very high opinion of that gentleman, after which two other couples followed, chiefly younger people, the host himself bringing up the rear with the wife of the archdeacon.

As soon as the company had taken their places, the archdeacon, in compliment to his rank, was asked, or rather, at a signal from the host, bent forward to say grace, which he did in a sort of half-inaudible, hasty singsong, as if in a hurry for the good things that were to follow, after which the covers were removed and the dinner was commenced.

With the politeness and good-breeding of a gentleman, and the courteous gallantry of a soldier, our hero could not fail to make himself agreeable to his fair companion, who received his attentions with a sort of half-sentimental bashfulness, as if she took it for granted that they were intended to be understood as the commencement of a serious love-making. It was evident that Mrs. Day, who sat on his right, wished to put the same construction upon his attentions. But she was a woman of too much experience and finesse to show the satisfaction she felt at the thought of entangling so eligible a match for her daughter, though every now and then there was a kind of half-patronising air in her tone and manner toward him, just sufficiently perceptible to show that she understood what was going on, and sufficiently formal to encourage his attention by a little apparent reserve, which was no doubt meant to increase rather than check the latent sentiments she appeared to fancy were entertained by William Haverty toward her daughter, who was himself utterly unconscious of any other feeling toward her than those engendered by his own natural cheerfulness of disposition, and a desire to please, which he would have equally felt toward any other young lady whom he might have been placed beside.

'Mamma tells me you are a captain now,' remarked Miss Julia Day in a low, half-timid voice, as if she were saying something she did not wish everyone else to hear, at the same time glancing half-languidly in his face.

'Yes, I have now the honour of holding that rank in her majesty's service,' he replied in a clear, unembarrassed voice.

'I am so glad to hear it,' returned the young lady, with a quiet earnestness. 'It is so pleasant, you know, to hear what one feels interested in, and has so much reg——' she was evidently on the point of saying 'regard for,' but abruptly paused and feigned to look a little confused.

'Thank you. Pray do not stop,' said William Haverty, with a half-amused not unpleased smile. 'I assure you I feel highly flattered and honoured by your interest and good wishes, especially as I was stupid enough not to know that I was so fortunate.'

'Oh, don't say stupid, captain,' returned the young lady, with a deprecating look. I'm sure no one can say that of you.'

'Well, it looks very like my being so, not to have known of such happiness as you inform me of,' he rejoined with a gay look.

'I am so glad you consider it so. But I m afraid you don't mean it. You gentlemen say such flattering things to us poor girls, and then laugh at us for believing you,' she said with artful innocence.

'I assure you I do mean it. I do indeed feel both flattered and happy at knowing I am fortunate enough to possess an interest in your thoughts and a share in your good wishes.'

'Ah! that's what you all say, you know.'

'Well, I am glad to know we have grace

enough in us to be grateful for such kindness on the part of the ladies.'

'Ay, but I mean you all say that, without meaning it,' she replied reproachfully.

'I am afraid your opinion of us is not so favourable as I was beginning to flatter myself it was,' William replied with a look of half-laughing disappointment. 'It was too bad of you, now, and very unkind too, to first excite one's vanity and then reduce one's self-esteem in that way.'

'Do you always mean everything you say, then?' inquired Miss Day, with well-feigned innocence.

'Of course I do. You don't doubt it, do you?'

'Oh, I don't know. We are always inclined to—to trust those we—we're—I mean we have known for some time,' said Julia, with some embarrassment, glancing half-fondly at her companion, who really, after all, began to feel somewhat interested in her.

'Well, I'm glad you feel inclined to make some exceptions to such a severe general condemnation,' rejoined William, 'and I hope I am one of the number you include under the amnesty.'

Miss Day, as if she considered this almost

equal to a declaration of love, affected to look confused, slightly blushed, and glanced at her mother, who, without appearing to do so, had heard every word of the conversation, and had been watching almost every expression of our hero's countenance, probably imagining that his easy politeness and attention really indicated those feelings in him toward her daughter, which it was the aim and desire of both the young lady and herself to inspire and cherish. Nor was she the only person in the room who narrowly watched and tried to hear what passed between William Haverty and Miss Julia Day.

The elder Mr. Ingram, although apparently far too much absorbed in his own self-importance and the dignity of his position to notice anyone at the table but the host, the archdeacon and his wife, the county-court judge and his wife, his partner Mr. Day, and one or two others, who were occasionally honoured by a stiff, pompous bow or a formal bend of the head; still, every now and then he cast a half-curious watchful glance at Captain Haverty and Miss Day, and evidently regarded, for some secret reason of his own, the polite attention of the former to that young lady with much internal gratification;

at such times, too, his eyes and those of his son, who was sitting a little lower down at the opposite side of the table to William Haverty, would meet with a half-cunning expression of mutual understanding, which showed that they clearly understood each other, and that they considered the *tête-à-tête* between Captain Haverty and Miss Julia Day as something that might be turned to account, in something that they felt interested in themselves.

'Well, I hope you will do us the honour of calling at Sunnydown House soon, Captain Haverty,' said Mrs. Day in her insinuatingly polite manner of assumed friendliness, as she shook hands with him at parting that evening after the dinner.

'Oh, certainly. I assure you I shall have great pleasure in calling in a day or two.'

'We shall all be glad to see you,' said Mr. Day, at a glance from his wife, for in matters of politeness or domestic diplomacy he was entirely under the guidance and control of his clever managing wife.

'Thank you. I shall not fail to avail myself of your kind invitation,' returned our hero, politely.

'Good-bye, Mr. Haverty,' said Miss Julia

Day, holding out her hand as she was about to step into the carriage, after her father and mother; for the latter had contrived that she should not only enter the carriage last, but that Captain Haverty should have the privilege of handing her in. 'I am so much obliged to you for your kindness and attention. Good-bye,' she repeated with a half-regretful glance up in his face, as he took hold of her hand and pressed it as she entered the carriage,

'Oh, don't say that. It is I who ought to thank you for the pleasure you have afforded me this evening,' he replied, though without betraying any of the sentimentality that might have been expected. 'I hope I shall have the pleasure of seeing you again in a day or two.'

'We shall all be so delighted to see you,' returned the young lady with modest earnestness, as she took her seat beside her mother, with her father facing them; and with a friendly bow from each, the carriage drove off, and our hero returned to the house and joined his father and mother, who were now ready to take their departure also.

A day or two after this, Captain Haverty paid his promised visit to Sunnydown House, which was about a couple of miles from his father's residence. It was a bright sunshiny day, with the robins chirping upon the bushes and the blackbirds hopping about among the shrubs, and a flight of starlings chattering and fluttering over each other upon the large lawn in front of the house, round the bottom of which lawn were a number of pines and lofty elms, with a few of last year's crows'-nests still upon them, as he walked up the broad circular carriage-drive to the door.

The windows of all the principal rooms in the house being front, it not only enabled the family at all times to see a visitor before he arrived, but also gave them time either to prepare for his reception, or have a 'not at home' ready in case of not wishing to see him.

Having rung the bell, Captain Haverty was immediately shown into a handsomely furnished room, where he found Mrs. Day, who, in spite of her pretended look of pleasant surprise, was evidently prepared for his visit.

'Captain Haverty!' exclaimed Mrs. Day, rising from her erect posture upon a low chair by the side of the fire, and gracefully holding out her small hand as he approached.

'How do you do? I am so glad to see you. —James,' said she, calling to the livery-servant who had shown him in, 'desire Miss Julia's maid to tell her mistress that Captain Haverty is here.'

'Yes, mum,' said the footman, as he left the room.

'My eldest daughter, I am sorry to say, will not be able to have the pleasure of seeing you, I am afraid, this morning,' said Mrs. Day, with a look of resignation.

'I am grieved to hear it; but I hope she is not in any danger.'

'Oh no, not at all; but you know, she is always so delicate, and very seldom can leave her own room,' returned Mrs. Day, with more cheerfulness.

Mrs. Day was not particularly well-informed upon either historical or geographical matters, and in the short conversation that followed made one or two rather uncommon mistakes as to the position of the Crimea—which she called *Crimmea*—the extent of the Russian empire—whether Sebastopol was a city, an island, a sea, or a continent; and had likewise rather confused notions respecting not only the chief incidents of the war, which she, out of compliment to her visitor, made some attempt to talk upon, but also as to the belligerents themselves, and the side England had taken in the quarrel; all of which she might have avoided had she acted with her usual tact, and not spoken of what she was ignorant.

She was, however, anxious to amuse her visitor, and introduced those topics rather with a view of gratifying his *amour propre* than that she took much interest in them herself, by paying a few delicate compliments to his gallantry, and offering her congratulations upon the honours he had achieved in the struggle.

It must be confessed that the few minutes her visitor had the honour of talking with Mrs. Day did not tend to increase his respect either for herself or her mental endowments; for beyond the few twaddling commonplaces, and the insipid gossip usual in the small cliques and circles of provincial society, she had few topics to entertain one who felt little or no interest in those things; while her affectation of extreme gentility of manner, as well as the wondrous friendliness which she professed for him, rather led William Haverty to doubt the sincerity of her character altogether. Her elegant vivacity, too, was more that of a young girl than that of an elderly lady, and her professed interest in him was rather that of one who wished to please or flatter her listener than of a real well-wisher.

However, beyond thinking that much of what she said was mere conventional flummery, William Haverty did not feel inclined to judge too harshly of her, and was willing to believe that she really had some satisfaction in receiving his visit, albeit her artificialness rendered it very difficult to discover what was really genuine and what was assumed.

Just as Captain Haverty was beginning to grow a little tired of Mrs. Day's rather uninteresting conversation, the footman returned to say that Miss Julia's maid had told him to say that her young mistress had just gone out into the garden; but if Mrs. Day wished, she would go and let her know that her mamma desired to see her.

'Perhaps you would like to take a stroll through the garden, Mr. Haverty?' said Mrs. Day. 'You are sure to find Julia there, or in the conservatory, which you will see behind the house. It may amuse you; and I know she will be so disappointed if you don't go and see her flowers. She is so fond of flowers, you know. I am very sorry I cannot have the pleasure of accompanying you, as I have a slight cold, and am afraid to go out; but, if you like, the footman shall show you the way.'

'Oh no, thank you. Perhaps I shall only disturb Miss Day in some of her floral operations if I go, and she would not like to be brought away from them.'

'No, not at all,' exclaimed Mrs. Day, almost alarmed lest he was going to propose going away without seeing her daughter at all, and the nice little romantic scheme concocted between them as they saw him approaching the house was going to fall to the ground; for it had only been a sudden thought of the young lady's to rush upstairs, seize a straw hat and feather, with turned-up sides, put on an elegant little cloth jacket with wide sleeves, loose body, and large buttons in front, and make her exit by a door which led out of the house into the garden behind, while he was talking to her mother, in hope that he might, under pretence of seeing the flowers in the conservatory, be induced to go and seek her there.

'No, not all,' said Mrs. Day; 'she is quite delighted to have some one, capable of appreciating them, to show her flowers to, and I know she will be so pleased to show them to you. But, if you would prefer not going out, I will send the servant to ask her to come in.'

'No, pray don't do that,' replied her visitor. 'If you think she won't be offended at my intruding upon her, I shall be very happy to go and find her in the garden.'

'Intruding!' said Mrs. Day, with an assuring smile; 'she will consider it a great honour and kindness on your part, and will be so glad to see you.'

'Thank you. I shall do myself the pleasure of going out, then.'

'Would you prefer going alone, or shall I send the servant with you to show you the way?'.

'Oh, not at all. I shall find my way very easily, I daresay,' he replied, rising.

Mrs. Day rang the bell, and desired the footman, who instantly answered it, to show Captain Haverty into the garden.

'You will, of course, have lunch with us before you go?' said Mrs. Day, with an insinuating politeness.

'Thank you, but I hope you will excuse me in that,' he said, as he prepared to follow the footman into the garden—' as I want to make another call,' he added, straining his conscience.

'Well, I don't know that I will,' returned Mrs. Day, with a smile; 'but we shall see when you come in.'

Without offering any further remark, the captain followed the footman out of the room, and was led across another room with a large bay-window opening upon a small flight of stone steps leading into the garden, which he descended, and strolled along the nicely-gravelled walk, with neat boxwood edges, towards the conservatory, which he saw close before him, adjoining the other end of the dwelling-house.

CHAPTER IV.

OBSERVING the door slightly open, Captain Haverty entered the conservatory and looked around him, but, for a few seconds, saw no one there. It was a long, roomy place, raised against a high, north wall, with glass roof, sides, and front facing the south, and long rows and tiers of sloping shelves raised above each other for the flowers, among which were several fine camellias, azaleas, hyacinths, and numerous other equally beautiful flowers, many of which were already in bloom.

The extreme beauty of the sight, and the delicious perfume of the flowers, fell upon him like a spell, and he stood looking around him and inhaling the sweet fragrance, utterly unconscious of everything but the delightful sensation created by the bright objects and pleasing odours by which he was surrounded.

However, he had not stood long when he heard a slight sound, as of a suppressed cough, somewhere in the place, and, the next moment, caught a glimpse of a lady's dress among some large plants and shrubs at the other end of the conservatory.

Walking towards the spot, he saw Miss Julia Day stooping down, with her back to him, partially concealed by a large white camellia, just coming into bloom, with a small bright trowel in her hand, and gloves on, apparently very busy putting some fresh mould to some young plants in small pots before her, and seemingly quite unconscious of the presence of anyone else.

Just as he had approached within two or three paces of her, the young lady gave a slight start, looked up, dropped the trowel, sprang to her feet, and, pulling off her gloves, hastily commenced smoothing down and dusting the front of her wide skirts with her pocket-handkerchief, with a look of pleasant surprise and confusion.

'Oh, Captain Haverty!' she exclaimed, holding out her small plump hand, and slightly blushing. 'I was so surprised, and

I am quite ashamed to be seen by anyone in such a trim.'

'Pray, Miss Day, don't say that. I think it looks charmingly appropriate,' said he admiringly; 'and becomes you so much,' he added, glancing at the picturesque attire, which, in such a place, certainly did look by no means inappropriate or unbecoming, as the artful little Julia right well knew, and displayed her plump, small figure, round face and small feet to the best advantage, which she also knew as well, or perhaps better, than he did.

'Do you think so?' she inquired with a coquettish smile. 'But you always compliment me so, you know.'

'Only when it is deserved, I assure you. You look quite charming, and among all these beautiful flowers and delicious scents, too!'

'I am sure you don't mean it; for I know I look quite frightful in this dress,' she returned with much scarce-concealed satisfaction, and glancing artfully innocent up in his face. 'Is not this camellia beautiful?' she asked, pointing to the one which had at first partially concealed her from his view.

'It is indeed. You have a very fine collection here. I was quite struck with the beauties and sweetness around me when I came in. But I am afraid I have intruded upon you,' he replied apologetically.

'Oh no! I assure you I am so fond of the flowers myself that I am quite pleased to get some one to come and see them. Are you fond of flowers?'

'Yes; very. I admire everything that is fair or beautiful.'

'So do I,' returned the young lady, feigning to look non-comprehensive of the implied compliment intended for herself, though evidently not a little pleased with it.

'Mamma told you I was here, I suppose,' she remarked after a short pause.

'Yes; the servant said you had gone out, and were either here or in the garden; and Mrs. Day asked me to step out and see you and the flowers at the same time.'

'But it was too bad of mamma to send you to find me in this trim.'

'Not at all. I am quite pleased to see you in such a picturesque dress.'

'Are you?' she inquired with a half-fondly serious glance.

'I am indeed.'

'Ah, I see you're only quizzing me,' she

rejoined, as if disappointed at not seeing stronger indications of passion in his look.

'No, I assure you I am not. Why are you so suspicious of my sincerity?'

'Because you don't look serious when you say these things.'

'Indeed! Then my looks are not a good index to my feelings; for I have not said anything that I don't mean,' replied the captain with rather more warmth, which she evidently accepted as an indication of regard, for there was a slight tremor in her voice as she rejoined:

'But you men can conceal your sentiments and thoughts so much better than we can. And do you really mean all those nice things you have said?' she asked with earnestness and artful simplicity.

'Why, yes, Miss Day,' he returned, somewhat surprised at the anxiety of the young lady to be assured of his sincerity in the trifling things he had said to her.

'I am not Miss Day, you know, Mr. Haverty,' said she, with another half-fond glance. 'I like best to be called Julia. Don't you like the name?'

'Yes, I think it is a very pretty one; so I shall call you Miss Julia, if you prefer it.'

'Oh no, I don't like to be called miss at all; I hate it. It's only what a parcel of tradespeople or servants call one.'

'But I am afraid it would be taking a liberty; I am not entitled to use so familiar a mode of address as that toward you.'

'Not at all. I should like it better than any other,' exclaimed Julia Day, persuasively. But come, let me show you the flowers in here, and then I'll show you the chrysanthemums in the garden, which are very fine this year. Isn't that a beautiful little heath there?'

'Yes, very; and so full of bloom too! What species is it?'

'It is called *Ericea regermonans*—or some such frightfully long word — or American heath. But is not it a shame to give things such dreadful names that one cannot pronounce them without stopping to take breath in the middle of it?' she inquired.

'Well, it is rather awkward sometimes, especially when that is the case,' he replied, laughing. 'But it is very beautiful, in spite of its name.'

'Yes, it is a very pretty specimen. But what do you think of this daphne? isn't it lovely?'

'It is indeed; the scent, too, is very delicious!'

'I am very fond of the daphne and the deutzia too. They are so beautiful, I think!' said the young lady, laying her hand gently upon one of the last named elegant shrubs, already coming into bloom.

'Ay, that is very beautiful!' said William, with a look of admiration. 'It is exceedingly elegant and graceful!'

'It is called the *deutzia gracilas*—I suppose on that account.'

'And a most appropriate title I think.'

'They used to call me deutzia when I was a child—not that I can fancy myself ever to have been at all like it,' said she, looking up with an air of the most knowing artlessness.

'If I might venture upon an opinion, I should say that it was very appropriate indeed.'

'For shame! I know you don't think so, but only say it to flatter me.'

'Upon my word I do, though,' he replied, with apparent seriousness. 'But is not it, as well as many of these others, very early?'

'Yes, they are almost too early. But the gardener has forced a good many of them on rather too much this year.'

'I thought so. I never saw either a daphne or a deutzia in bloom so early before. By-the-bye, how very like orange-blossoms the deutzia-flower is!' exclaimed her companion, smiling.

'Indeed! Do you think so?' said the young lady, with another slight blush, and a sentimental look, as if she thought this implied an allusion to something that it was only becoming for her to blush at.

'Yes, I think it is very like it indeed. And how charming you would look with a piece upon that hat of yours!' with rather more earnestness in his tone than he had yet displayed, as if the scene and the conversation, in spite of the little interest he at first felt for Miss Day, were gradually beginning to exercise their love-inspiring influence upon his heart.

'Oh, do you think so?'

'Yes, I do. Just let me try,' said he, breaking off a small twig, on which the bloom was pretty well expanded, and sticking it half-playfully in the front of her straw hat, while at the same moment a sudden feeling of remorse fell upon his heart, as if he felt he had carried this trifling rather too far, and must now cease; for although he knew the young lady to be a cunning little schemer, who had practised her arts and tried her charms upon half a dozen beside himself, he did not feel that this was sufficient to justify him in exciting hopes or sentiments in her that he had no serious intention of returning. The slight pang that this thought gave him made him let the piece of deutzia fall from his hand and drop upon the ground at her feet, while she looked up, evidently half-surprised and half-disappointed at the sudden change in his manner, as he immediately added: 'I beg your pardon, Miss Day. I have been very rude in taking such a liberty with you,' and he somewhat abruptly turned round as if to leave the conservatory. 'I'm afraid I have been very rude; but I hope you won't think I meant to be offensive.'

'No, not at all,' replied the young lady, as if unwilling to relinquish the advantage that she fancied she had gained. 'If you like, I will show you the chrysanthemums now.'

'Oh, thank you; but I'm afraid I am really tasking your politeness and patience more than I have any right to do,' he replied, somewhat indifferently.

'No, no—not in the least. I shall be very

happy to show you them, if you wish it,' returned Miss Julia, with rather less animation than before.

'Well, if it is not too much trouble, I shall be very glad to see them.'

'Oh, it isn't any trouble,' said she, leading the way out of the conservatory and across part of the garden to a large bed of those beautiful winter flowers, still in all the splendour of their full, bright colours of pink, yellow, scarlet, and white.

'They are very beautiful,' he remarked, as he stopped before them, with an admiring look.

'Yes, they are generally considered very fine,' said his companion, who seemed to feel that the brief spell she fondly dreamed had fallen upon his heart was already broken.

'I am extremely obliged to you, Miss Day, for all this kindness and attention, and hope you will forgive me for—for the trouble I have given you; and for my intrusion upon you,' he replied, rather confusedly, and with rather more formal politeness than he had used in the conservatory.

'Pray don't mention that, Mr. Haverty,' said she, trying to conceal something like chagrin as she spoke. 'Only I am sorry to have detained you so long looking at my flowers, when I dare say you don't care for them, and would much rather have been somewhere else ?'

'I hope you don't think that, Miss Day ?' he returned hastily, and slightly colouring as he caught her cunning blue eyes fixed upon his countenance. 'I assure you I have been very much amused and interested; and am greatly obliged to you for the pleasure you have afforded me.'

By this time they had reached the stone steps which led from the garden into the house, and following his fair conductress, he again returned to the room where he had previously seen Mr. Day, with whom he now found Mr. Day, and Mr. Ingram, who both rose as they entered.

'How do you do, Captain Haverty ?' said Mr. Day, shaking him cordially by the hand. 'I am glad to see you, and hope you have been amused with the flowers in the conservatory and garden.'

'Thank you, I have indeed,' he replied, with a slight look of embarrassment which was most probably entirely misunderstood.

'Well, they are very pretty, I believe; but I seldom see them myself. My daughter, here, looks after them.'

'How do you do, Mr. Haverty?' said Mr. Ingram, in a sort of affected tone of lofty politeness, holding out the two forefingers of his right hand, which the captain courteously took hold of and returned his 'How do you do?' 'I am glad to—to see you, and I hope I may have the pleasure of congratulating you on—on the pleasure you have derived from the society of your fair cicerone among the flowers,' added Mr. Ingram half-craftily, glancing with affected humour at the young lady, who certainly did not look quite so well pleased with our hero as she did at first.

'I have been very much pleased; and am greatly indebted to the kindness of Miss Day for the pleasure I have enjoyed.'

Courteously, but steadfastly declining Mr. and Mrs. Day's pressing invitation to stay lunch with them, which he was informed was just coming in, Captain Haverty wished them good-morning and left the house, scarcely over-well satisfied with either himself, or that Mr. Ingram should have seen him return from the garden and conservatory with Miss Julia Day, in case his object in being there should be misunderstood either by that gentleman or the parents of the young lady themselves.

CHAPTER V.

CAPTAIN HAVERTY's dissatisfaction with himself for his foolish flirtation in the conservatory with Julia Day, only increased as he left the house and pursued his way towards his own home. He felt that he had not only been guilty of imprudence, but of real unkindness to that young lady, who, however artful and designing she and her mother might be to secure a husband, had certainly done nothing to justify him in trifling with her feelings, or treating her with discourtesy; and even if she had, it was contrary to the usual generosity of his sentiments to cause needless pain to any one, more especially to a young lady who, after all, he believed had many amiable points in her character, and was not without a good deal of agreeable attraction; and had she by any chance appeared before him at that moment, he would have endeavoured to atone for his cruelty and injustice —for he felt as if he had been guilty of both—by a free surrender of himself to their feelings and influence. Fortunately, or, perhaps, unfortunately, for both, she did not appear, and in another moment the thought was chased away from his mind by the recollection of Blanche Wyndham.

What! Could it be possible that he had, even for an instant, allowed the idea of another to usurp her throne in his heart? He shrank from the mere thought with something akin to secret horror; and the bitterness of that moment might well have atoned for his recent folly with Julia Day. Nor did it lessen his secret vexation as he was approaching the road which turned off towards the residence of the Wyndhams, to see Mr. Ingram ride up from an opposite direction and enter the house.

Captain Haverty had no doubt but the chief object of that gentleman's visit there was to inform the Wyndhams of what he had seen, and of course magnify his attentions to Julia Day to suit his purpose in assisting the schemes of Mr. James Murray. His mortification as he thought of this was extreme, and he bitterly regretted the folly that had exposed him to the misrepresentation of others, as well as the reprehension of his own conscience.

And what would Blanche Wyndham think of him when she was told of his conduct, which he felt confident she would be? Would she not feel that he was not only unworthy of any further regard, but also of the affection she had previously cherished for him? And would she not feel that he had left her to her impending unhappy lot with Mr. James Murray, while he was resolved to seek his own happiness elsewhere, without making a single effort to rescue her from her coming fate, or to prove to her the strength and purity of his affection?

Absorbed and depressed with these painful thoughts, our hero walked on and reached home in much lower spirits than he had experienced for some days, and sat down in his own room to indulge in his sorrowful emotions by himself. He had not, however, sat long when Patrick O'Brien, who had seen him come in, tapped at the door, and said that his father wished to see him downstairs.

On descending to the sitting-room, he

found General Fielden there, who had only a few minutes before entered.

'How do you do?' said the general, rising and shaking him warmly by the hand. 'I am glad to see you looking so well, and so much stronger since you came home. I hope you enjoyed yourself at my house on Friday.'

'Yes, thank you, very much indeed,' replied William, rather less animatedly, perhaps, than the general expected.

'I am glad to hear it. I thought you would, with the lovely little companion I managed to assign you for the evening. You and she seemed to get on very well together, I thought,' said General Fielden, smiling good-humouredly. 'But I hope you have not already resigned your heart into her keeping.'

'Oh no! I'm afraid she would think it very lightly won, and prize it accordingly, if I were to resign so quickly as that,' he returned, with a forced laugh.

'Well, that is fortunate, as I fear you will soon be called upon again to buckle on your armour and fight for our country.'

'What!' exclaimed Captain Haverty, with a start, in an instant throwing off all selfish depression and grief from his heart, like Samson casting from him the snapped cords by which his enemies had sought to bind his mighty strength; 'has this patched-up peace, made to suit the convenience of our ally the Emperor of the French, been broken already?'

'No, that rather unsubstantial fabric still stands; but I'm afraid a much mightier one is upon the point of being assailed.'

'Indeed! You don't mean that we have quarrelled with our friend Louis Napoleon, and are likely to turn round and fight the French, after having joined with them to fight the Russians?'

'No, that eventuality is only an eventuality still, I am glad to say, that is, as far as I am aware, at all events, for my information does not refer to that.'

'What in the name of goodness then is it?' exclaimed William Haverty, half impatiently. 'We are not going to war with the Yankees, I hope?'

'No, nor yet going to kill the *Turkeys* for our own use, that you lately had such trouble in protecting from the Russian Bear,' replied the general, laughing.

'Well, if they were all killed to-morrow, it would be little loss to either humanity, civilization, or the world,' returned William; 'for a more worthless race of lying rascals I never came in contact with. But what is this news you have, general?'

'Well,' he replied, with a grave look, 'I have just had a letter from an old friend in India, who gives me a most gloomy account of the state of things in the army there; and says he is as firmly convinced there will be a mutiny among the native troops before three months go over, as if he had seen it already, and that nothing can either keep them in order or preserve the country but a large increase of European soldiers, which he believes will shortly be made. He says he only hopes that this may be done before the outbreak takes place.'

'Then I hope the Ninety-third will be one of the regiments sent to quell them, or keep them in check, as the case may be,' said the captain, with great fervour, as if struggling with some secret feelings of his own, and hoping for relief in renewed action.

'I noticed by the *Times*, which I received just as I was coming out, that the Ninety-third is one of the regiments likely to be sent to India soon, for the purpose of increasing the European army there.'

'But, if the danger of an outbreak is so great, the Government ought not to talk of sending out troops soon, but order them off at once,' remarked William Haverty, almost impatiently.

'Perhaps they don't think that the danger is so imminent, and that there is plenty of time.'

'And be too late with everything, and sacrifice thousands of lives to their obstinate stupidity, as was done in the Crimea,' remarked Colonel Haverty bitterly.

'That's not unlikely, colonel,' replied the general. 'But,' he added, after a moment's pause, 'having seen in the paper that your regiment was likely to be sent to India, I hastened along to let you know, in case you had not heard of it.'

'I had not heard anything of it, though we had some idea ourselves that we might be sent out before long.'

'Then you mean to join your regiment and go out, I suppose?'

'Yes, I am quite fit for service again, and will go with the regiment wherever it is sent. I only hope that if we do go we shall have old Sir Colin Campbell with us.'

'I am almost afraid his age might prevent

his going out to India again,' remarked the general. 'I have not seen him for more than twenty years; but he's an old man, and, like you and I, colonel, he must be beginning to feel old age pressing rather hard upon him!'

'Not a bit,' exclaimed the colonel heartily. 'My son tells me our dear, old, dashing young friend of five-and-twenty years ago is almost as active now as he was then.'

'What a wonderful old man he is, to be sure!' remarked General Fielden admiringly.

'Ay, he is indeed; and if my dear boy,' said the colonel, with a sudden break and huskiness in his voice, 'does go to India, I pray God it may be under the command of Sir Colin Campbell.'

'Do you think he is likely to go in case of the Government wishing him, William?' inquired the general.

'I believe, as far as his age is concerned, that would be no impediment at all, and as far as his energies and abilities are concerned, there is no man that the regiment, or the army itself, would so soon see as its leader; but whether he would be disposed to go or not, I cannot so well give an opinion: though I believe if his services are really required he would not hesitate to go anywhere that the exigencies of the country required; for he is as tough as steel and as brave as a lion,' he added, with enthusiastic admiration.

'Ay, he's a noble fellow,' returned General Fielden. 'But your father has just told me you wished to see me about something. You know, as far as my services and influence are of use, they are at your command. I hope,' he added, with a smile, 'it is not another case of frightening my worthy brother magistrate, Mr. James Murray.'

'No, not at all: it rather relates to your own interests than mine,' he replied, and as briefly as he could he related the conversation between Mr. Ingram and Mr. Murray that he had overheard in the Bank, and expressed his own opinion of the insecurity of any money that was in the hands of the partners of that establishment.

'You quite surprise me,' remarked the general, who had listened with great attention to the recital, and not without considerable uneasiness in his look. 'Why, I always thought Ingram and Day's bank almost as safe as the Bank of England itself.'

'And so have a great many others, and I dare say they do so still,' replied William.

'But for all that I have very strong doubts upon the subject.'

'Well, I confess I am somewhat inclined to take your view of it. It certainly does not look well; and that visit, too, of Mr. Ingram's to your father, is anything but straightforward, I think. And you, colonel, promised to let him have the use of the money for some time longer?'

'Yes,' replied the colonel, wincing.

'Well, I am very sorry you did. Is it a large sum?'

'A good deal for me, as I am not a very rich man, and have three children,' returned the colonel, with a forced smile. 'It is about three thousand pounds.'

'I wish mine hadn't been more,' said the general, gravely. 'It is over twenty thousand.'

'Indeed! twenty thousand pounds!' exclaimed his old friend. 'Perhaps you hold some security?'

'No, indeed, I do not. Do you?'

'I wish I did. I have only the acknowledgment of the bank.'

'That, too, is all I have,' thoughtfully replied the general.

There was a short, uneasy pause.

'This is, I am afraid, a rather serious affair, colonel,' remarked the general, at length breaking silence.

'*You* think it is?'

'I do indeed. I fear so, at any rate. Don't you?'

'Well, I confess the more I think of it, the more uneasy I feel.'

'So do I. But what do you mean to do?'

'I really feel as if I could not do anything; I have, in a manner, pledged myself not to withdraw the money at less than six or nine months' notice; and having so recently told Mr. Ingram that I did not wish to have it at present, I don't see how I can ask him for it now. What do you intend doing?'

'Well, I hardly know. I shall, in the first place, try to ascertain something more about the position of those people, and endeavour to get some security for my money, if I even allow it to remain; otherwise, I shall withdraw it. Though I believe I must give six months' notice, too, before I can do that. It is really a very delicate and unpleasant thing, to have to do this with people that one has been on terms of intimacy with so many years; although, I confess, the Ingrams and Days have always appeared to assume far more importance than their position entitles them to, and I shouldn't wonder but all this great show of theirs, with their fine houses and parks, grand parties, carriages and horses, and splendid establishments, and expensive families, has been entirely supported by other people's money. And that such a shallow, pompous old man as that Ingram should have the impertinence to talk in the way he seems to have done of both you and myself, as if we were merely tools in his hands, to be used as he thinks fit, for his own purposes and objects, is a presumption that I do not at all feel inclined to allow him to entertain,' continued the gallant general, with rising indignation. 'But to some extent we deserve it; at all events I do, I fear, for having so long tacitly yielded to the assumptions of him and his family.'

'Well, he always thought himself far too grand a man to take much notice of a poor old soldier like me, who has little beyond his pay and his pension. But knowing you were a man of large property, he thought it more worth his while to pay you a little attention, I suppose.'

'And for that has made a tool of me,' rejoined the general, indignantly.

'Let us hope not,' said the colonel, trying to assume a more hopeful look and tone; 'it may not be so bad, after all, as we imagine.'

'It may not, certainly; but I confess I have very strong fears upon the subject. 'What do you think, William?'

'I hardly know what to think, and am almost afraid to venture an opinion. I only wish that I may be mistaken in what I have already said upon the subject.'

'Well, both for my own and your father's sake, I wish the same, though I fear you are not. But do you really mean to let your money remain in their hands, after what your son has said, Haverty?' asked the general, turning to his old friend.

'I can't see what else I can do. Could you, as an old friend, and a man of the most susceptible honour yourself, advise me to do otherwise?' inquired Colonel Haverty, gravely.

'No; if you have really promised to give him the notice you mention—though, of course, you are perfectly well aware, a mere promise of that kind is not legally binding; and I doubt if he would keep it with you, if it suited his purpose not to do so.'

'Perhaps he would not, but I feel myself

that I could not go from the promise that I have made, without doing an injury to my own sense of honour.'

'I dare not advise you in the matter. I know your honourable nature too well to try to induce you to do anything contrary to it. Although, as I said before, there is nothing legally binding in such a promise, and I have some doubts in my own mind, too, if under the circumstances you are morally called upon to respect it. But, of course, you will at all events immediately send in a notice to have the money ready for you six months from this time.'

'Do you think I should ?'

'Most assuredly, yes. You have no need to stand upon ceremony with either Mr. Ingram or Mr. Day, as you have fortunately been less intimate with them than I have been—an honour, I fear, I am likely to pay rather dearly for.'

'Do you think so, William?' asked his father, still looking reluctant to act so promptly. 'I know you wouldn't wish me to do anything, even to benefit yourself, that you thought contrary to the honour of a soldier and a gentleman, any more than the general ; and if you think I ought to do as he advises, I will. I am an old man now, and should be sorry to do anything that might make my family feel ashamed of me when I am gone ! But if you think I ought to send this notice to withdraw the money now, I will do it.'

'I dare not advise you in the matter, father,' said the son, whose honour was not less sensitive than his father's, afraid to second General Fielden's advice, lest it might have the appearance of looking after his own interest in the money more than his father's feelings.

'Come, now, general—for I have great faith in your judgment as well as your honour— tell me candidly, do you think I ought to withdraw the money ?'

'Yes, most decidedly,' replied the general, unhesitatingly. 'Your duty to your wife and family demands that you should endeavour to recover this money, and if you give the six months' notice that you promised, that is all that can be required to satisfy the most sensitive honour in the world.'

'Then I shall do so,' said the colonel, looking as if a weight had been taken off his mind. 'But what do you propose doing ?'

'Well, as I have said, I shall endeavour to find out something about the bank, and see if they can give me any security for my money, in the first place; and then act according to circumstances. But if I find the safety of the bank is at all doubtful, or that they cannot give me security for my money, I shall then withdraw it as quickly as possible. Only we must be careful not to do anything either to excite their suspicion or that of other people, as that would only render the probability of our getting our own money all the more uncertain, and might also do them an injury, which I should be sorry to do, although that infamous scheme of Murray's to deceive Mr. Wyndham and to secure the fortune of poor Blanche, which it is evident the Ingrams are assisting him to carry out, does not entitle them to merit either respect or consideration from honourable men. I am heartily sorry for that poor girl, and cannot understand the blindness and folly of her father and mother in trying to force her to marry a man for whom she evidently cares nothing, and who has no regard for her except for her money, and a man, too, who is by no means likely to make either a kind or a faithful husband.'

'I fear not, from what I have heard,' said

the colonel, quietly, while his son turned to the window and stood looking out upon the lawn in front of the house, to hide his feelings from their observation.

'Cannot anything be done to open Mr. Wyndham's eyes to the real condition of Murray's affairs, and the prospects of his daughter if she marries him?' said General Fielden, thoughtfully.

'I am afraid not. It is such a delicate thing for anyone to interfere in, or offer any advice upon, that I should hardly like to take the responsibility upon myself,' replied Colonel Haverty; adding in an under-tone, not to let his son hear, 'especially as it might be supposed I had some motive of my own in doing so.'

'Humph! I understand,' returned the other, in the same tone. 'Well, they can't think that of me, and for the sake of the young lady herself, if not for some one else, I shall try what I can do.'

'It would certainly come much better from you than from me; and for poor Blanche's sake I wish you may be successful in your efforts.'

'Then you will send in your notice to the bank at once, about the withdrawal of your money, I suppose,' said the general, preparing to leave, Mrs. Haverty having at that moment entered the room.

'What, have you prevailed upon my husband to take his money out of the bank, after all?' she inquired, looking half-wonderingly at the general.

'Yes, we have just been talking the matter over, and, considering all the circumstances, your husband thinks it desirable to send in a notice that he wishes to withdraw the money at the end of six months—as he seems to think his honour would be compromised if he drew it out earlier.'

'Well, I am just as well pleased, for I confess I don't like those Ingrams, nor Days either,' said Mrs. Haverty; 'but won't you have a glass of wine and a biscuit before you go?'

'No, thank you; you know I seldom take anything before dinner. Good-bye.'

The colonel and his son walked with the general to the door.

'I shall let you know the result of my inquiries, if I learn anything respecting those people,' whispered the general to the colonel, as William stepped forward to open the door, 'and also how I succeed in that other affair. Good-bye,' he added aloud. 'Good-bye, William. If I hear or see anything more about your regiment going to India, I'll let you know.'

'Thank you; I shall feel much obliged. Good-morning.'

And the general took his way homewards, with the intention of calling on the Wyndhams in passing.

CHAPTER VI.

'COLONEL HAVERTY presents his compliments to Messrs. Ingram and Day, and begs to intimate his desire to draw out the amount of money in their hands at the end of six months from this date, as he finds he will require it about that time.

'Colonel Haverty regrets to send this notice so soon after having informed Mr. Ingram that he did not require the use of the money at present; but circumstances which he did not then foresee or contemplate have arisen since he saw that gentleman, which render it necessary for him to call in the money sooner than he had calculated upon. He hopes, therefore, that Messrs. Ingram and Day will not deem him discourteous in sending this early note of his intention respecting the withdrawal of the money.

'BILFORD, *Dec.* 28, 18—.'

Having written the foregoing note to Messrs. Ingram and Day, Patrick O'Brien was despatched with it the same afternoon to the bank in Westdon.

'Is there any answer to come back, plaise yer honor?' asked Patrick, as the colonel gave the note to him.

'I don't know whether they will think it necessary to send any answer or not; but if Mr. Ingram or Mr. Day is there when you leave the note, you might just wait till they have read it, in case of their wishing to send a reply.'

'You know where to go, Patrick? The place where I left you outside when you were in the town with me the other day.'

'Sure an' I do, yer honor. The place, ye mane, where that gintleman, Mr. Murray, came out o'?'

'Yes.'

'Thank yer honor. I won't forget that,' said Patrick, in a tone of confidence, as he left the room.

A few minutes later he started, his stout elm stick, which he held by the middle, in his hand, every now and then twirling it round as he went along on his way toward Westdon, where he arrived in due course, and walked into the bank with the air of a man who is fully conscious of the dignity of his position, as well as the importance of his present mission.

'Is the masther in?' he inquired, addressing one of the two gentlemen behind the counter.

'Masther in? What do you mean, fellow?' demanded the gentleman, indignantly. 'What do you want?'

'I want to spake to the masther,' said O'Brien, repeating the offensive word.

'We don't talk about masters here,' returned the gentleman spoken to. 'Do you think we're a parcel of footmen, like you?'

'I mane no offence, young gintleman,' said Patrick, quietly. 'Only I want to spake to one of the masthers.'

'Well, there's no masther here,' replied the irate gentleman, trying to imitate the pronunciation of the Irishman.

'Indeed! Sure now, an' 'tis the first shop I ever saw that had no masther belonging to it,' returned Patrick, with a shrug of the shoulders.

'Now, fellow, you had better say what you want, or be off about your business. We cannot have the like of you loitering about the bank. Shop, indeed! Just like the impudence of you ignorant Irish!'

'Och! be aisy now, young gintleman, or it's myself that will be afther tachin' ye manners, an' not to be insultin' a man that comes from Colonel Haverty to lave this note wi' yer masther.'

Whether it was that he did not altogether relish the implied threat, or that, hearing the name of Colonel Haverty, the cashier thought it best to assume a more conciliatory tone, we cannot say, but he replied, more courteously:

'Do you mean Mr. Ingram or Mr. Day?'

'Sure, now, I don't care which,' said Patrick, with perfect indifference.

'Well, Mr. Ingram is within, if that is what you want.'

'Sure, now, an' why couldn't ye ha' tould me so afore?' said Patrick, half indignantly.

'Well, I tell you so now, at any rate. Do you want to see him?'

'Och, an' what else should I have asked for him for but that same?' exclaimed Patrick, highly amused with the question.

'Well, he's engaged,' replied the clerk, turning to a desk at one end of the counter, and beginning to write in one of the books which were lying upon it.

'Och, then, I'm in no particular hurry,' said Patrick complacently, taking possession of a seat which was against the wall facing the counter, and commencing to amuse himself by looking round the cornices and up at the ceiling. After he had sat for some time the other cashier spoke to him.

'If that letter in your hand is for Mr. Ingram, you had better let it be sent in to him before he goes home, or you may wait here long enough before he's able to see you,' said he, glancing up at the clock, which was over the door, as if to intimate that it was near the time that Mr Ingram generally left.

'It's for either Mr. Ingram or the other gintleman, Misther Day,' replied Patrick. 'But you can give the despatch to Mr. Ingram,' he added, holding out the note with a half-reluctant air, as if unwilling to trust it out of his sight, having the idea that he was to deliver it himself to one of the principals of the bank.

'Stay there, then, and I'll bring you the answer, if there is one,' said the clerk, going into Mr. Ingram's private office, closing the door behind him.

Mr. Ingram was sitting at a flat office-table with a small, slightly raised writing-desk before him, his chin supported in the hollow of his left hand, with his elbow resting upon the front of his desk. There were writing materials, some open letters, and various other papers lying upon the table, and a small, partially open fire-proof iron safe in the wall behind him, in which Mr. Ingram kept his own private papers.

'A note from Colonel Haverty,' said the clerk, putting it down before him, and pausing to hear if there was any reply or message.

'Eh, from Colonel Haverty!' replied Mr. Ingram, with a half-startled look. 'Humph! what does he want?' he muttered, trying to assume an indifferent tone before the clerk. 'Anyone waiting?' he inquired, breaking open the envelope.

'Yes, sir; his servant, I believe it is, who brought it.'

'Very well; I shall ring if there's any reply to go back.'

There was a slight tremor on Mr. Ingram's lips, and an expression of mingled surprise and vexation in his face, as he hastily ran his eye over the note. For a minute, after reading it, he sat biting his lower lip, as if to check his feelings, with a look of puzzled anxiety and anger. At length he suddenly touched the ivory nob of a small spring-bell which stood before him, and, on its being answered by the clerk, inquired if Mr. Day was within.

'Yes, sir. He has just come in, and is in his private room.'

'Ask him if he will be so good as to step in and speak to me for a minute or two,' said the banker, scarcely looking at the clerk.

'Yes, sir,' and he left the room.

In two or three minutes Mr. Day entered.

'Just read that,' said Mr. Ingram, handing the note to his partner, who read it over with a look of astonishment and chagrin not less than it had occasioned Mr. Ingram.

For a few minutes there was a blank pause, as if both were alike puzzled and at a loss what to say; at length Mr. Day spoke:

'This is very awkward. I wonder if he has heard anything to cause him to wish to withdraw his money.'

'I am really puzzled as much as you to make this out. I cannot see how it is possible that he can have heard anything; and yet it seems very extraordinary, after what he told me when I saw him the other day.'

'It does indeed! You don't think, then, that it is merely the prospect of wanting the money himself that has induced him to write this note?' remarked Mr. Day.

'No; I do not. Yet I am perfectly at a loss to understand how he can have discovered anything to make him do it for any other reason. Although, I confess, I have been rather uneasy upon that point since that son of his drew out his remittance, for he could not possibly require the whole of it at once. But the chief question for us to consider is, what we are to do, as the colonel's servant, I believe, is waiting for an answer.'

'It is very awkward to have to pay out so large a sum, considering the difficulties of our present position. To be sure, he gives us the six months' notice you mentioned; but even then I doubt if we shall be in any better position to do it than we are now,' said Mr. Day.

'I doubt it too; and yet something must be done, for if people once get alarmed, we shall be ruined.'

'I fear so. I really don't know what to do. And yet, as you say, something must be done, in case Colonel Haverty has found out anything that has shaken his confidence.'

'Yes; for if he has, and General Fielden hears of it—the colonel is sure to tell him—and calls in his money, that would stop us at once.'

'We must counteract that by some means or other, and that speedily too,' said Mr. Day. 'I see you have your private ledger open. What balance have we in hand now?'

'Not much, I am sorry to say. Barely enough to pay Colonel Haverty. A thought has just struck me that the best means we could adopt would be to let him have this money at once. That would be the most likely way to disarm General Fielden of any suspicion he may have received through the Havertys,' replied Mr. Ingram.

'That's just what I was thinking myself; and if it could be done, I almost think we ought to try it. The impression created by such prompt repayment of his money would be most desirable.'

'Well, we have about two thousand pounds' worth of bills due to us, which will no doubt be paid to-morrow, as well as one or two other things, which will bring up our funds a little; and unless we have unusually large drawings, there would be enough to meet them and pay the Havertys also—and I really think we ought to try it.'

'So do I.'

'But, if we do, I'm afraid we must stop

our advances to James Murray for a time,' replied Mr. Ingram.

'We had better do that than risk our own credit. It will only cause him to postpone his marriage with Miss Wyndham for a time. Only we must take care that we do it in a way that does not excite his suspicions as to the real cause.'

'Yes, I can manage that well enough. And it would, too, give us relief in another way: as Murray will have to put off his marriage for a month or two, Mr. Wyndham will not want the five thousand pounds he told us of for some time either.'

'True; and that's another screw removed,' returned Mr. Day, brightening up. 'Then by all means I should recommend that we let Haverty have his money now, instead of waiting till the six months expire.'

'Then we had better write him a note to say so. Will you do so, or shall I?'

'Oh, which you like.'

'Well, I don't want to write to the old fellow—confound him! Suppose you do it,' said Mr. Ingram, complacently.

'Humph! I will write. I suppose we had better not show any surprise or uneasiness at the purport of his note.'

'Our best plan is to appear perfectly civil and unconcerned. But you may as well take my seat and write your answer here,' said Mr. Ingram, rising, and laying down a sheet of note-paper and an envelope upon his desk, at which the other sat down and wrote as follows :

'Messrs. Ingram and Day present their compliments to Colonel Haverty, and in reply to his favour, intimating his wish to withdraw the amount they hold belonging to him in six months, if equally agreeable to him, they would much prefer his doing so at once. The money is therefore at his command ; and Messrs. Ingram and Day will be happy to hand it to him to-morrow, if he will either call or send for it.
'The Bank,
  'Westdon,
    'Dec. 28, 18—.'

'There, what do you think of that ?' inquired Mr. Day, handing the note to his partner. 'Will it do ?'

'Yes, only it's much too civil for the confounded old Irishman.'

'However, I think it is best to seem perfectly civil and polite. It would be unwise, I'm afraid, to show anything like vexation or uneasiness,' replied Mr. Day.

'Quite right. If that doesn't astonish the old fellow, and dispel his suspicion, I'm much mistaken,' said Mr. Ingram, confidently.

'There's nothing else you could suggest that would be better, is there?' asked Mr. Day, preparing to put the note in the envelope.

'No, nothing. I don't think it could be better.'

Again touching the spring-bell, which was directly answered by the clerk, as before, Mr. Ingram took the note his partner had written, and desired it to be given to Colonel Haverty's servant, who was waiting in the bank. As soon as O'Brien received it he took his departure, and made the best of his way toward Bilford.

CHAPTER VII.

GREAT was the astonishment of both Colonel Haverty and his son when they found that the money, about which they had been so uneasy, had been so promptly placed at the colonel's command by the bankers; and their first thoughts were a disagreeable kind of sensation that they had conceived, and been entertaining, unjust suspicions respecting those gentlemen, and had, probably, even done them injury in the estimation of General Fielden. This was a thought which was anything but gratifying to the generous nature of either the father or his son, and they resolved to lose no time in trying to repair it as far as they could.

'Well, William, it would seem that we have made a mistake, after all,' remarked the colonel, as he laid down the note.

'It certainly does look so,' replied William, musingly; 'and yet I cannot believe that I misunderstood what I heard between Mr. Ingram and Mr. James Murray. Still, I confess, this promptness of theirs makes me almost doubt my own thoughts and suspicions of the bankers; and I am sorry now that I said anything to General Fielden about it, as no doubt he must feel very uneasy, having so large a sum in their hands.'

'Yes, it is almost a pity we did say anything to him; and we must endeavour to see him as soon as possible, and let him know the result of my application for the money. We owe this to the bankers themselves, as well as to the general,' returned Colonel Haverty, grieved no less to think that injustice, as he supposed, had been done to Messrs. Ingram and Day, than that unnecessary fears had been excited in the mind of his old friend respecting the safety of his money.

'I will walk to the general's this evening, and let him know the answer you have received to your note,' said the son, after a moment's pause.

'I think you had better, William. You are

pretty certain to find him at home in the evening, and the sooner you see him the better.'

Waiting till he thought General Fielden would have finished his dinner, William Haverty took his way to inform him of the answer his father had received from Messrs. Ingram and Day, taking their note to his father with him.

'Well, this doesn't look as if your suspicions were very correct,' remarked the general, with a thoughtful smile, when he read the note; 'and they don't seem to be at all offended either, or as if they imagined your father wished to withdraw his money from any doubts as to its safety in their hands, which is all the more in their favour.'

'No; it's a very civil note indeed. Had they appeared at all angry or surprised, or shown any unwillingness to comply with my father's request, I should have been not only more confident that I was right in my suspicions, but better pleased with what I had advised my father to do; for one doesn't like to be treated so courteously by people one has an unfavourable opinion of.'

'Then you still have an unfavourable opinion of them?'

'I allude rather to the men than the bankers in this, for I confess to anything but a high estimation of either of the Ingrams or even the Days, especially the former.'

'That scheme of Murray's to deceive Mr. Wyndham, in which Mr. Ingram seems to be assisting, is a most disgraceful piece of business, and has very much lowered the latter in my estimation. As for the former, he could hardly be lower than he was before, especially since the *fracas* with you. But I hardly know what to think about this other matter. I suppose your doubts are quite dispelled upon that point.'

'No; they are not altogether gone, even now. It may perhaps be that I have conceived a wrong opinion, or that a feeling of something like personal dislike prejudices me against them, even in this respect; but, I confess, I have still a vague kind of suspicion that they are unsafe people to trust one's money with. The few words that I overheard between Mr. Ingram and Mr. James Murray, the day I called at the bank, have left an impression on my mind that I cannot quite get rid of.'

'Sometimes those kind of half-instinctive feelings are the truest after all,' said the general, in a musing tone; 'at all events, I shall so far act upon your impressions, that I shall try to find out how far the bank is safe, and, under any circumstances, endeavour to get them to give me some security for my money.'

'My father and I thought it was only right to both you and Messrs. Ingram and Day to let you know the result of his application at once; as we feared we might have made you uneasy without any occasion for it, as well as have done them an injustice.'

'Thank you. You are very kind. I confess I was rather uneasy; nor is it altogether dispelled by this note of theirs to your father. But you ought not to have so bad an opinion of them either,' he added, with a smile.

'Why, general?' he inquired with a slightly wondering look.

'Why, I've just heard that you are paying your addresses to Mr. Day's youngest daughter.'

'Indeed!' said William, with a confused look which probably the general construed into proof of the truth of the assertion.

'Yes; I mentioned that I was going to call on the Wyndhams after I left you and your father this morning; and was told so there,' replied the general. 'Ah, you sly one! You didn't tell me when I saw you that you had just returned from a visit to that charming little damsel,' he added banteringly.

William Haverty's mortification at hearing this prevented his being able to reply for a few seconds.

'Never mind,' continued the general, in the same tone; 'you needn't change colour so, as if you were frightened to hear it. If you don't want me to talk about it, I will not; only I had some doubts about its being true when I heard it.'

'I hope you do not think it is true,' at length he stammered, with more of vexation than sentiment in his tone.

'Why, what else am I to think? Your looks certainly betray something like guilt; and it seems Mr. Ingram told the Wyndhams only a few minutes before I was there to-day that he had seen you at the Days' this morning, where you had been courting Miss Julia in the garden or conservatory, among the flowers.'

'But surely the Wyndhams did not believe this!' said William Haverty, with considerable agitation in his voice.

'Believe it! What else were they to do?

Mr. Ingram said he saw you and the young lady returning to the house while he was there ; and that Mrs. Day herself had told him of your attention to her daughter, to which neither she nor Mr. Day are disposed to offer any opposition—that's so much consolation for you.'

'It will be quite soon enough for Mr. and Mrs. Day to express their approval when I ask them for it,' replied our hero, curtly.

'Why, you don't mean to say you don't intend asking their approval?'

'I have not the slightest intention of ever doing so, for the simple reason that I never intend placing myself in a position to require it. But I deserve this for my folly,' he added bitterly, 'though I had no idea that a simple call, especially after the pressing invitation of Mrs. Day when I met her here, could have been regarded by her in such a light.'

'Humph! I know Mrs. Day is rather a match-making lady, and is said to be anxious to secure husbands for her daughters. But how was it you were so long in the conservatory with the young lady, if you were not making love to her?'

'I should not for a moment have supposed that my going into the conservatory, especially after having been pressed to do so by her mother, could have been construed into any intention on my part to pay my addresses to Miss Day, either by herself or anyone else; or I certainly should not have gone, or even called at the house,' replied our hero, who felt impelled to say something to clear himself in the estimation of the general.

'Then you do not mean to lay siege to the young lady's heart? Of course, I've no business to inquire, only, as I am an old man, as well as an old friend, I may be allowed, I hope, to be a little curious, which I assure you arises much more from the interest I take in you than from any other cause.'

'I assure you, sir,' he replied, with respectful regard, 'if I had any intention of doing so, I should not hesitate in not only telling you, but of asking your advice; but I have not the slightest.'

'Well, I am obliged to you for your confidence. But it's very foolish of Mr. Ingram, as well as very wrong, to try to spread a report that there is so little foundation for, and which might be injurious to both you and the young lady in question—especially to her, for unfounded rumours of that kind are always injurious to ladies; though it would appear her mother is even more foolish in the matter than he is.'

Of course she was. But General Fielden did not know that Mrs. Day fancied that, by assisting to do this, she was aiding the scheme of Mr. Murray to marry Blanche Wyndham, by making that young lady believe William Haverty had given up all thoughts of her, when the said Mrs. Day deemed there would then be more chance of securing him for her own daughter, after Blanche had been consigned to another; or that Mr. Ingram, whose interest in the matter merely consisted in certain secret objects of his own respecting the property Mr. Murray was likely to receive through his intended wife—knowing the still strong regard cherished by Blanche Wyndham for William Haverty—had called upon the Wyndhams that morning for the very purpose of informing them of the circumstance, which he very much exaggerated, of having seen the captain at the Days' that morning, and what Mrs. Day told him upon the subject of his visit. Though General Fielden did not suspect this, William Haverty did; and it was a thought that gave a deep pang to his heart, confirming as it did, or seemed to do, his belief that Blanche Wyndham must have heard of his visit to Sunnydown House, and no doubt been led to believe he had really given her up.

This, however, he resolved should not be. He determined—if it were only to prove to her he had not forsaken her, although she had advised him to forget her—that he would take some means of either seeing her, or of communicating with her, to clear his character from the inconstancy which, in her estimation, might now be attached to it. And as he passed Bilford Hall, on his way home from General Fielden's, his heart swelled with mingled indignation and grief, as he thought that, at that very moment perhaps, Blanche Wyndham might be listening to the repetition of the story of his unfaithfulness to her, and his now bitterly repented visit to Sunnydown House.

CHAPTER VIII.

Next morning Colonel Haverty went into Westdon and drew out his money from Messrs. Ingram and Day's bank, and, for the better security, placed it in another bank in the town—which was known to be perfectly safe—till such time as he could find a good investment for it.

Shortly after his father left for Westdon, William Haverty went out for a walk upon the heights, and, in his way home, strolled along a lane which led past the house of the Wyndhams—for that was the centre round which his thoughts still revolved—probably hoping he might see some one connected with the family of whom he might learn something about Blanche. But such hopes, if he had them, were doomed to disappointment, for he passed the house and returned home without having seen anyone belonging to it.

Restless and unhappy, he went upstairs and sat down before the fire in his dressing-room, which he also used as a kind of study. Anxious, as he was to communicate with Blanche Wyndham, and to convince her that, whatever she might have heard respecting his visit to the Days, he was still true to the dream of their youth, however hopeless it now was, he could not, after the letter he had received from her, forbidding his doing so, write to her, or take any other means of conveying any message to her: and yet something within him seemed to urge him to do so. It might be a desire to vindicate himself to her, or a feeling of hope lingering in his breast, or probably both. Still he could not prevail upon himself to make any effort to open a correspondence with her, although his withholding himself from it was rather the result of habitual self-restraint and mental discipline than of his own inclinations, but even in this he was far from satisfying either his own feelings or his sense of duty to her under the circumstances in which she was placed. Perhaps his pride, as much as his conviction that what he was doing was right, impelled him to resist the longing of his heart to seek once more an interview with her. But, be it as it may, after sitting brooding upon the subject for more than an hour, he was still unable either to form any plan of communicating with Blanche Wyndham, or any resolution to overcome the influence she still exercised over his heart and feelings. Thus several days passed, and weeks followed days, during which he continued to struggle with his feelings, and haunt the solitary lanes with the same indecision and the same unsatisfactory result.

Nor was Blanche Wyndham less unhappy during this time. Although she had advised him not to reply to her letter, or try to see her, she had scarcely hoped that he would abide by it, and immediately afterwards regretted she had done so. But when she heard of his visit to Sunnydown House, and of his attentions to Julia Day, which had been duly detailed to her by her mother, after Mr. Ingram's call, she felt more than ever sorry for the prohibition she had placed upon him, believing that it might possibly have had something to do with his so suddenly seeking to forget her in the society of another.

Knowing that the most li' ' means of

persuading her to look upon James Murray with less reluctance than she had hitherto done, was to weaken her respect for William Haverty, Mr. Ingram had taken care to insinuate into the minds of both Mr. and Mrs. Wyndham anything but a complimentary opinion of him, as well as a much exaggerated idea of his attention to Julia Day, leading them to suppose that he must have cared very little for their daughter to transfer his affection so speedily to another. This they had duly repeated and enlarged upon to Blanche, who was forced, to some extent, to believe it—especially as he had taken no means of assuring her of the contrary.

Her pride now came to her assistance, and she resolved to smother or conceal her own secret feelings, and to assume an air of greater hopefulness than she had worn for many a month past, even though her heart should burst in the struggle. Not only was Mr. Murray, but her parents, greatly pleased with this, regarding it as a hopeful sign that their efforts to win her appreciation of her approaching marriage had at length been successful; although, had they been as anxious to discover her real feelings as they were to see those that indicated compliance with their wishes, they could hardly have failed in observing that, in spite of all her efforts to appear cheerful, she would often burst into tears without any apparent cause, and sob with a violence of grief and a desolation of look that nothing could pacify or dispel; at which times, if Mr. Murray chanced to be present, she would shrink from him with the most intense aversion, and display the greatest disgust of his person. After which she would, as it were with a great effort, throw off her emotion, and crush back into her own swelling heart the aversion she had to her intended husband, and try to appear pleased with his formal attentions, and more compliant with the wishes of her parents.

In the meantime, Messrs. Ingram and Day having informed Mr. James Murray that they could not at present supply him with any more money for the furnishing of his house, he had been compelled to postpone his marriage for a time on that account; without, of course, acquainting the Wyndhams with the particular reason, or rather assigning to them as the reason of the delay the inability of the tradesmen to have the house ready so soon as he had expected.

When this was told Blanche Wyndham,

she heard it with comparative indifference. She had now almost ceased to hope for any escape from her impending union with James Murray, and had become, in a manner, careless as to when the ceremony took place: yea, even at times almost wishing that it were already performed, if it were only to escape from her present state of gloomy foreboding of anticipated wretchedness.

During this interval, General Fielden had endeavoured to find out if his money was really safe in the hands of Messrs. Ingram and Day, but had failed to discover anything either to confirm his suspicions or to restore his confidence. He had, therefore, taken an opportunity of calling upon those gentlemen, and hinting to them his wish to have some other security for it than their mere acknowledgment, which was all he had hitherto held.

At first they showed considerable surprise, and even betrayed some uneasiness; but they quickly assumed their usual crafty composure, and without any apparent hesitation agreed to give him the security he required, which they did by giving him a bond for the amount, signed by themselves. From the great confidence that everyone seemed to have in their bank, and the promptness with which they had met Colonel Haverty's application, as well as the friendly feeling that had so long prevailed between him and those gentlemen, which he was unwilling to disturb by unnecessary precautions, General Fielden deemed this enough, believing that, after all, the remarks upon which William Haverty had founded his suspicions might either have been misunderstood by him, or perhaps used only by Mr. Ingram to cover his unwillingness to advance more money to Mr. Murray.

Be that, however, as it may, the general, without ever once thinking that this was not a whit better security than what he had before, accepted it, though he resolved to exercise a certain degree of watchfulness, and to give notice of the withdrawal of his money the moment he saw any real grounds for doubt or suspicion.

During this time, too, William Haverty had received an invitation from Mrs. Day to a party at Sunnydown House, which he had self-denial enough to decline. He had not sufficiently overcome the mortification of his last visit, and the construction that had been put upon his motives, to venture a second time into the company of either the scheming Mrs. Day or her husband-hunting daughter.

Often and often had he strolled past Bilford Hall, and once or twice he had seen Blanche Wyndham at church with her father and mother; but, except a formal bow when he chanced to meet them, he had never been able either to make up his mind to call upon them, or to speak to them when they met. And, no other opportunity having offered, he had still been unable to find any means of communicating with Blanche, or of ascertaining the real state of her feelings toward him. But this was now about to be given him.

One evening, about this time, he was sitting in his dressing-room, after the rest of the household had gone to bed. He happened to cast his eyes towards the window, fancying he had seen something like a flash of lightning shine through the blind for a moment and then disappear again in the darkness. At first he thought little of it, except, perhaps, that it was rather unusual to see lightning at that season of the year, and sat listening for the thunder that he expected to follow it. But no peal came. In a few seconds another flash rose up; not, however, to disappear like the previous one, but to continue bright and glowing like a mighty column of distant fire. Wondering what it was, he rose from his seat, and turned the blind aside to look through the window, when, to his astonishment, he saw a large, dense body of flame ascending into the dark night, and lighting all the country for some distance around. It happened that the windows looked in the direction of Bilford Hall, and he at once saw that the fire was either there or close to it.

For a few moments he stood watching it, and then, fearful that it was Bilford Hall itself, he quietly pulled on his boots, which he had already taken off, and noiselessly went downstairs, where he put on a cloth cap, buttoned his coat, and cautiously opening the door to avoid alarming his father and mother, he went out, closing the door gently behind him, and hastened off in the direction of the fire.

The instant he gained the open air he saw that the fire must be at Bilford Hall, and every step he took only increased his fears for the inmates of the house. On he rushed, and arrived at the gate leading from the road to the front door just as a large volume of flame and smoke burst through a window which he well knew was on the first landing on the principal staircase. Several people were already there, and the sound of feet was already heard in all directions approaching the house; but no engines or means of extinguishing the fire were at hand, or could be had nearer than Westdon.

Just as he arrived at the door, the first person he saw was Mrs. Wyndham, who was standing held by a couple of female servants to prevent her rushing into the house in search of her husband and daughter. Close to her stood Mr. James Murray, with his hat on and his riding-whip in his hand, as if he had only just arrived, or had been upon the point of starting from the house when the discovery of the fire was made, with several countrymen all clamouring and running to and fro, but quite incapable of doing anything either to check the fire or aid those who might require their assistance.

'Where is Mr. Wyndham? and where is Blanche?' exclaimed Captain Haverty, in a moment throwing off all reserve.

'Oh, William!' cried Mrs. Wyndham, wringing her hands in frantic grief. 'They're both in the house, and here are the people all staring about, and none of them trying to save them. Oh, Mr. Murray!' she exclaimed imploringly, 'can nothing be done to save my poor daughter and my husband? You ought not to have stood by and seen him go in search of her without going with him to help him!' she said in a half-reproachful tone. 'Let me go! If I cannot save them I can at least share their fate!' she cried, again struggling to break from the servants.

'I—I—' began to stammer Mr. Murray, evidently a good deal excited, but sufficiently cool to keep himself out of danger, and looking for a moment as if about to make some exertion, and then suddenly shrinking back again. 'I—I—fear——'

'Good God! Are they in the house, and you standing here?' cried our hero, scarcely looking at either Mr. Murray or those around him.

'Yes, they are upstairs,' replied one of the servants, who was beside her mistress, whom Captain Haverty instantly recognised as Eliza Fleming. 'Oh, sir, try to save my poor master and my dear young mistress!' she added, with intense earnestness.

'Ay, that I will, or perish in the attempt!' he cried, dashing forward toward the staircase, taking the precaution to snatch out his silk pocket-handkerchief and throw it over his head and face.

As if the countrymen had been shamed into momentary courage, or only wanted some one to lead them, three or four went on a few steps after him; but when they saw the terrible flame that was raging before them, which had already caught hold of the stairs, they paused, shrunk back and left him to proceed alone, while Mr. James Murray continued lingering near the outer door, as if ready to make his exit in case of any danger to himself.

At this moment, however, a man dashed in at the door, and, without pausing for an instant, followed Captain Haverty up the flaming staircase. It was Patrick O'Brien, who, having heard the door close when his master went out, had jumped from his bed, and, seeing the red glare in the dark sky, had hastily thrown on his clothes and slipped out of the house by the back-door, and made for the scene of the conflagration, where he arrived a few seconds after his master.

On went William Haverty, bounding up the stairs, and quickly reached the landing at the top, rushing from room to room in search of Mr. Wyndham and Blanche. Knowing the house pretty well, he had no difficulty in finding his way, although the smoke, which now filled every corner, and the fast-encroaching rush of the flames, rendered his progress extremely dangerous. Still he thought of nothing but of those whose lives he was resolved to save, and dashed through flames and smoke as if he had been impervious to their influence. Once or twice he paused and listened, but could hear neither voice nor sound to indicate where Mr. Wyndham and Blanche were. He shouted, but there was no answer. Still he pursued his search, flying from room to room, utterly regardless of his own danger from the rapidly increasing fury of the fire.

At length, after he had gone through all the principal bedrooms on both the first and second floors, and paused for a moment in an agony of despair at the top of the first stair, to which he had again returned, all of which had not occupied him more than a few seconds, he saw a door at the opposite end of the passage which he had not before tried, knowing that it led into a wing of the house over the kitchen, and, he believed, belonged to some of the servants. But resolved to search every corner of the house till he found those he sought, he instantly made toward this door, which unfortunately was now almost cut off by the fire that had caught hold of the flooring in the passage, and rendered it a matter of not less danger than difficulty to get to it.

Without, however, a moment's pause or hesitation he dashed through the flame, and burst the door open, when to his relief he found both Mr. Wyndham and Blanche, although in a condition that almost dispelled his first joy at finding them.

Blanche Wyndham, on the first alarm of the fire, had hastily dressed herself, and tried to make her escape downstairs, but had been driven back by the flames, and sought shelter in this room, where her father, after seeing his wife out of danger and in the care of the servants, had a few minutes afterwards found her, but only to find that the spreading fire had cut off their retreat. Knowing their only chance of escape was in keeping the fire from the room as long as possible, Mr. Wyndham had closed the door and thrown the small window open, in hopes of attracting the notice of some one outside, and obtaining assistance by that means; but, although a great number of people were now assembled, they were all at the other side and front of the house, so that his shouts had been all unheard, and nothing seemed now before them but an appalling death; and in their despair they had again closed the window to prevent the draught from drawing in the flames.

When William Haverty entered the room he found them both almost exhausted; and so dense was the smoke that it was scarcely possible to breathe. Blanche Wyndham had just thrown herself upon her knees, imploring her father to leave her and try to save himself, when he sprang into the room and closed the door behind him to keep out the flames, which seemed to pursue him, as if in vengeance of his indifference to their rage. Seeing they were both almost fainting for fresh air, he hastily opened the window, which Mr. Wyndham had closed, and with a strength which men only have in such moments of terrible emergency, carried first Blanche and then her father to it, shouting again, with all his might, for help from outside.

Just at that moment, Patrick O'Brien, who, with a courage only equalled by that of his master, had followed him through all the devious windings and rooms of the house, now losing sight of him for a few seconds and then catching a glimpse of him again amid the smoke and flames, as he flew from room to room in search of Blanche Wyndham and her father, dashed into the room after him.

'For God's sake, masther!' he exclaimed, 'don't stay here. Ye'll be burned to death in two minutes if ye don't escape!'

'Escape, Patrick!' replied his master, surprised to see his servant there. 'What do you mean? Do you think I can seek my own safety and leave these to perish in the fire?'

'No, plaise yer honour,' said Patrick, who never, even in the greatest danger, forgot the respect due to his master; 'but if yer honour would try to get back before the fire reaches here, and laive me to take charge o' the lady and gintleman while yer honour sends assistance to us by the window, it would be betther——'

'No, Patrick, I shall remain; but do you go back if you can, and let some of the people know where we are, and tell them to bring ladders, if there are any, to the window Quick! there's not a moment to lose,' said the captain, while Patrick, with a reluctant glance, sprang round and opened the door to make his escape, if possible, by the passage again. But it was too late. A large portion of the floor had already fallen in: and the flames, which were now within a foot of the door, feeling the fresh current caused by the opening of the door, leaped up in his face, singeing his hair and eyebrows, and driving him back into the room. With a quick effort he again closed the door, and, without speaking, turned to his master, who saw the danger they were in too well to require to be told it.

William Haverty's next thought was to rush to the window to see if there was any possible means of escape by it. But although the height would not have prevented him from jumping down himself, it was too great both for Mr. Wyndham and Blanche, who were still, though breathing more freely, in a state of semi-insensibility.

Fortunately, at this moment, Patrick saw a small wash-stand in a corner of the room, with a basin and jug of water upon it. Quick as thought he brought the water forward and dashed a portion of it in the face of the young lady and her father, which had the effect of partially reviving them.

'Good God, Patrick! can nothing be done to save them? Oh, that we could get any of the people outside to see or hear us! But they are all at the other side of the house,' said the captain, with terrible concentration of anxiety. 'See! see! the flames are now coming in at the top of the door! In five minutes more it will be all over with them and us!'

'Not if Patrick O'Brien can help it, yer honor,' replied the servant, stripping off his coat and pushing it firmly into the space that the fire had already made in the top of the door, thereby checking it in that spot for a few moments, and then approaching the window as if to spring out, casting a scrutinising glance down upon the dark ground, indistinctly seen fifteen or sixteen feet beneath him. 'Does yer honor know what's below?'

'Only the garden ground, I believe.'

'Do not attempt to go out there,' said Mr. Wyndham, rousing himself from his half-unconsciousness. 'You'll only break your limbs, or perhaps your neck, without saving us. What, William! Are you here to perish with us? Oh, my child! my poor child! I could have borne it, but for you!' he shrieked, looking at his still scarcely conscious daughter, who — roused from her lethargy by the agonised voice of her father, and probably, too, at hearing the name of one who was once, ay ! and who was still, so dear to her—made a feeble effort to push her father toward the window, as if to show her desire for him to try to save himself, and then, clasping her hands together, sank upon her knees, with an expression of mingled composure and holy earnestness, which went to the heart of William with a power that no words can describe.

' Quick, Patrick !' said the captain, seeing his servant about to go out of the window which he had already torn from the frame. ' Don't jump, but get out, and give me hold of your hands, and then you can drop down with less danger of hurting yourself ; and bring ropes, or ladders, and lights, if you can find them, as speedily as possible !'

' But wouldn't yer honor rather get out, an' laive me here till you can fetch assistance ?' urged Patrick.

' No, Patrick ; I remain here till I have seen these two persons safe, or perish with them ! So away for help before it's too late !'

' May God and the holy Virgin keep you and them !' replied Patrick, fervently, as he got upon the window-sill ; and, after hanging by his hands for a moment, let himself drop quietly and steadily down by the side of the wall.

'How is it, Patrick?' inquired his master, anxiously.

'All right, yer honor,' he replied cheeringly, as he regained his feet, for he had been thrown upon his back by something he came in contact with in his descent, fortunately without doing himself any serious injury. 'Don't be uneasy, sir. I shall save ye, or die with yer honor, if that's any gratification,' as he rushed off round the end of the house to procure assistance.

During this time, although it had not occupied more than a very few minutes, the agony of poor Mrs. Wyndham on account of her husband and daughter was intense. But for the determined resistance of her servants and those around her, she would herself have rushed in amid the flames in search of them. Great, therefore, was her joy and that of the crowd when Patrick O'Brien appeared to them with the intelligence that they were still alive, although in the most imminent danger. In a minute a couple of ladders were procured from an outhouse, torches were kindled, and some half a dozen of the more daring of the men who were standing round volunteered to assist O'Brien in his difficult and dangerous task.

In the meantime the flames had again burned through the door of the room, caught the floor, and were making the most rapid approaches to where William Haverty stood, near the window, partially supporting Blanche Wyndham, who had now sufficiently revived to stand, with his and her father's assistance.

'Never mind, Blanche,' said he, quivering with emotion, and feeling as if it would be happiness to perish with her, but speaking in a cheering voice; 'we shall have assistance in a moment.'

'Oh, William!' she exclaimed entreatingly, 'do not remain here to perish! Save yourself, and, if possible, save dear papa!'

'We shall all be saved, dear Blanche,' he replied tenderly. 'Oh that Patrick would come!' he muttered to himself, with intense earnestness, as he saw the roaring flames every moment coming closer and closer to them.

'I fear all help is now in vain, even if it could be obtained,' remarked Mr. Wyndham, despondingly. 'If I and my daughter are doomed to perish in the flames, God's will be done! But you, William, are young and strong and active, and may perhaps jump from the window without much injury to yourself. Go, then, and leave us to die by ourselves; and may God reward you for the danger you have already encountered on our behalf!'

'No, Mr. Wyndham, I shall not leave here till you and Blanche are safe. Look! Thank God! here they come!' he exclaimed, as he saw a crowd of people with ladders and torches coming round the corner of the house, amongst whom was Mrs. Wyndham, who could not be restrained from following. Among the throng, too, at that moment appeared a grey-haired old gentleman, who forced his way to the front, and was about to rush up one of the ladders, when Patrick O'Brien slipped past him, sprang up the steps, and in another instant was inside the room.

'Now, plaise yer honor,' cried Patrick, addressing his master, 'will ye go first and save the lady, and laive me to bring down the gintleman?'

'Oh! save my daughter! Never mind me. If I do perish, it's of little importance;

only save my child!' cried Mr. Wyndham, vehemently,

'Och, yer honor, an' it's mysilf that manes to save ye both,' replied Patrick, at the same time, seeing that he would not move till his daughter was safe, assisting his master to get Blanche up to the window-sill, when the next moment William sprang beside her, while O'Brien, quickly fastening the end of a shawl which she had over her shoulders, round the neck of his master, so that she could not fall back without pulling him with her, held them both steady till the captain had got his feet firmly upon the ladder.

A loud cheer rose from the crowd below as William Haverty swiftly, but steadily, descended the ladder with Blanche Wyndham. The silk handkerchief, although much burned and singed, was still about his head and face, and partially concealed his features, so that, except one or two that knew who it was, very few recognised him.

'What! William Haverty?' exclaimed General Fielden, in astonishment, as he saw him descend and hand over Blanche Wyndham to her mother and some of the women about her; 'how in Heaven's name did you get in there? God bless, you my boy! But are you all safe?'

'All right, thank you, general,' he replied quickly; and turning again, sprang up the ladder to help Patrick with Mr. Wyndham, whose danger was now of the most appalling kind. A second ladder had been raised, and another man had gone up as far as the window; but the scene that met him there, made him shrink back. Except a small space close to the window upon which Patrick was partially supporting Mr. Wyndham, the whole room was a bright roaring flame, and several sparks of fire had already fallen upon their clothes.

Mr. Wyndham had again become almost incapable of standing, and O'Brien himself was nearly suffocated. Fortunately, at this moment, some of the people below approached with pails and cans of water, in the hopes of extinguishing the fire by that means. In an instant William Haverty saw the necessity of reviving both Mr. Wyndham and his own servant before making any attempt at getting them out, and rushing down the ladder seizing hold of one of the pails and bounding up with it, dashed it full in their faces, which had the effect of not only instantly reviving them, but of checking for a moment the rush of flames towards them. Seeing this, the man upon the other ladder did the same; while at the same moment Captain Haverty sprang in amid the dense smoke, which now came out darker than ever, and, with the assistance of his servant, succeeded in getting Mr. Wyndham upon the window-sill.

For a few seconds there was a silence, still as death, among the anxious people below. Each one held his breath in the terrible suspense of the moment.

'Quick! quick! The flames have caught the top of the window-frame,' cried General Fielden, in a tone of constrained emotion and energy.

'O God! They'll be all lost yet! My husband! my poor husband will be burned before my eyes!' shrieked Mrs. Wyndham, who, now that she knew her daughter was safe, had concentrated all her thoughts upon the danger of her husband, and stood looking at his perilous position with the most intense agony and terror, holding up her trembling hands and struggling to go to his assistance.

'Never fear; Captain Haverty will save him yet,' said the general, speaking very low and with the most intense earnestness, as he saw the dangers to which all the three were exposed. 'Hold fast the ladder underneath there,' he added, as he saw Patrick O'Brien get out, and, after some difficulty, get Mr. Wyndham upon his back and begin to descend.

Cautiously and slowly the brave fellow felt his way down the ladder, holding on by it with one hand and keeping Mr. Wyndham fast with the other; while, utterly regardless of the flames which were now almost upon him, William Haverty continued bending out at the window, and holding the top of the ladder till Patrick O'Brien with his load had got more than half-way down, when, just as a shout was upon the tongues of the people, ready to burst out, the ladder broke and both tumbled down, amid a cry of terror from the assembled crowd. Fortunately they had not far to fall, and were apparently little injured. But this accident not only destroyed our hero's only chance of escape, for the second ladder had already been removed to leave the space the clearer, but for the moment turned the people's attention from the frightful danger of his position also.

In an instant, however, General Fielden saw it, and called for the other ladder to be brought. But before this could be done, the captain, who was almost choked for want of fresh air, and whose dress was already on fire in two or three places, had once more got upon the window-sill to make his escape, which was now a matter of the most imminent danger and difficulty, as the wood-work was now nearly all on fire, and his hands were so much burned that he could neither use them freely nor drop himself down, as Patrick had done previously, without great risk to his limbs and person. However, feeling that anything was better than being burnt alive, he prepared to make the attempt.

'Steady, William! Stand clear there! Hold on a moment—here is some straw,' cried General Fielden, and one or two other voices, as a man—probably in anticipation of such an emergency — brought a large bundle of straw, threw it down for him to alight upon.

Steadying himself for an instant as well as he could, William half leaped and half dropped from the window, and alighted rather heavily upon the straw, slightly stunned by his fall, in his present state of exhaustion. Nor was his danger over yet, for he had no sooner touched the straw than the fire which was upon his clothes set it in a blaze; so that it was with the greatest difficulty he could be extricated from it, and the flames sufficiently extinguished to allow any one to touch him. Still neither his consciousness nor his presence of mind for a moment forsook him; and when he found the straw had caught fire, he instantly rolled himself off it upon the ground, and continued rolling to and fro till, with the assistance of General Fielden and one or two of the bystanders, the fire about him had been put out.

'And now,' said he, beginning to feel the effects of his late dangers and exertions, and also the scorching he had received, as he hastily threw off the remnants of the silk handkerchief which still hung round his neck, ' a little water;' but before it could be brought he had fainted, and was as utterly unconscious of everything around him, as if his life had for ever left him.

CHAPTER IX.

WHEN the ladder gave way beneath Patrick O'Brien, he had to sustain the whole weight of Mr. Wyndham, as they fell together to the ground. The height, however, being comparatively small, neither, as we have before said, seemed to have received any serious injury; and as soon as Mr. Wyndham had been removed from him he sprang to his feet, ready to rush back to the assistance of his master, while Mr. Wyndham was immediately carried off to the coach-house, under the care of Mrs. Wyndham and a few of the people, and laid upon some soft hay, a short distance from his daughter, who, attended by Eliza Fleming and two or three women, was just beginning to recover her consciousness; while Mr. Murray, who had for some minutes been lost sight of, now that the danger was over, came forward as if to offer his services and watch over the safety of his betrothed, who, as she slowly opened her eyes and saw him standing before her, seemed to shrink from his very look with a mingled feeling of contempt and indignation.

'If you please, Mr. Murray,' said Eliza Fleming, seeing this, addressing that gentleman in something like a tone of command, for she had never entertained much respect for him, and now it was less than ever; 'if you please, sir, I think you had better leave my young mistress at present;' adding, after a moment's pause: 'Them that kept out of the way when she was in danger of being burned alive, and couldn't do anything to save her then, don't need to come about her and disturb her after she is in my care.'

'Well, I hope, young woman, you will do your duty to her without chattering so much about things that don't belong to your position to interfere in, or to talk about,' said Mr. James Murray, with a confused look of ill-concealed anger as he walked, rather crestfallen, away, leaving Eliza Fleming and one or two other women, to attend to her young mistress, to the evident relief of Blanche Wyndham and her faithful attendant.

'Thank God he's gone! I only wish I might never see his face again,' muttered Fleming, between her teeth; at the same time observing a slight smile upon the pale face of her young mistress, which, however, almost instantly fled, while she slightly moved her lips as if trying to say something, but had scarcely the power to do so.

'Oh, but he is killed!' Blanche exclaimed, with terrible anxiety.

'No, he is not! He is only a little faint, and is already recovering.'

'Where is mamma? I know she escaped at first, but where is she now? Are you sure she is safe?' she asked, with trembling eagerness.

'Yes, my dearest child, I am quite safe,' said Mrs. Wyndham, approaching, and throwing herself down beside her daughter, embraced her with passionate earnestness and joy.

'Oh, is papa safe?' again asked the daughter, as soon as she could speak. 'You're sure he's not dead?'

'No, my dear. He is a little scorched, and has fainted; but General Fielden says there's no danger now.'

'And where is—is William Haverty?' she asked, trembling violently.

'He has been saved too!'

When she heard this, Blanche Wyndham fervently clasped her hands, as if she thanked God in her heart, but did not speak.

At this moment Mr. Wyndham, who had been laid down a few paces from his daughter, began to open his eyes; and, glancing slowly around him, failed, in the dim light of a solitary candle in a small lantern, to distinguish either his wife or Blanche.

'My wife! my daughter!' he muttered anxiously, with still only partially recovered consciousness; 'where are they? Has my daughter been saved?'

'Yes; they are both safe, and here,' said some one, in a soft, gentle voice, full of tender affection and solicitude, coming forward.

It was Mrs. Wyndham, who, hearing her husband's voice, had left her daughter to join him. At the same time, slightly assisted by Elizabeth Fleming, Blanche rose and approached him also, while all the three instantly joined in a deep, earnest embrace of overflowing affection.

'But where is he to whom we are all indebted for our preservation?' inquired Mr. Wyndham, gradually becoming more and more alive to surrounding objects. 'Where is William Haverty?'

Before any reply could be given, William Haverty was carried in and placed in the coach-house, in a state of insensibility. His case was by far the most dangerous, being very much burned, as well as bruised from his fall. Fortunately the doctor, who had seen the fire and had hastened toward it, hearing that some people had been carried into the coach-house very much injured, at that moment entered, and immediately commenced using every means in his power to restore him, while General Fielden stood by watching his operations with a look of the deepest earnestness and sympathy. Nor was Patrick O'Brien's the least anxious face there. Regardless of his own burns and bruises, his thoughts and cares were fixed upon his master, beside whom he sat, with all the tender devotion of faithful affection, assisting the surgeon in his endeavours to restore him to animation.

For a short time there was a deep, breathless silence. At length the surgeon muttered, half to himself: 'Thank heaven, he breathes at last!' which, though scarcely articulate, was sufficiently audible to be heard by those around him, and seemed to take a heavy load from every breast present as they drew in a long, deep sigh of relief, and gave a silent, hopeful glance at each other's face as they heard it.

Seeing that Mr. Wyndham had now observed him, General Fielden went forward, and taking him warmly by the hand, expressed his deep thankfulness and joy at his providential escape from his fearful dangers. The tears were in the gallant old soldier's eyes as he did this; nor was Mr. Wyndham less sensible of either his late danger or the general's affectionate interest, as he returned the friendly clasp of his hand.

In the meantime, a large number of people being gathered round the burning house, and a couple of engines having arrived from Westdon, strong efforts were now made to check the fire, which had hitherto raged with unopposed fury. But it was too late to offer any effectual resistance to the dread power of the devouring element; and in a very short time after Mr. Wyndham and Blanche had been rescued, the whole house was wrapped in flames. Nor were all the efforts made to subdue or check it of the slightest service, for in a short time the house and nearly everything in it had fallen a prey to the irresistible rage of the fire, leaving only blackened walls, charred wood, and smoking ruins, where a few hours before had stood a fine, elegantly-furnished house, full of life, comfort, and security.

With the foresight of a man accustomed to contemplate and prepare for every contingency, General Fielden had already despatched a messenger ordering his carriage to be brought immediately for the purpose of having the sufferers conveyed to his own house. In a short time it arrived, when he communicated his intention to the surgeon and Mrs. Wyndham.

'Oh, general, I cannot tell you how grateful I am to you for your great consideration and kindness to us in such a moment of trial as this.'

'Nay, never talk of that, Mrs. Wyndham,' he interrupted, with genuine sincerity; 'there's little merit in all that I have either done or even do. I hope you will consider my house as your home, and everything it contains at your command, not only till your husband and daughter are quite recovered, but till you have been able to find a fitting residence.'

'I am indeed grateful to you for your generous kindness, and most thankfully accept it; though I hope we shall not require to tax your liberality very long.'

'Don't talk of its being a tax, Mrs. Wyndham: for I assure you, I am only too happy to have it in my power to serve you at such an important time as this.'

'But what shall we do with Captain Haverty?' inquired Mrs. Wyndham. 'Will he be able to be removed, do you think?' she added, turning to the doctor.

'Not yet, I fear,' replied that gentleman. 'I do not apprehend any immediate danger, but I do not think it would be right to remove him for some time yet. He is quite safe and tolerably comfortable where he is, and I shall stay with him till he is able to be removed either to his own house or General Fielden's.'

'Well, if it were not that I'm afraid it would only increase both his own anxiety and that of his father and mother, I should have him taken to my house also. But that we shall decide upon afterward. In the meantime, you and Mr. Wyndham and your daughter shall be conveyed to more comfortable and convenient quarters; after which my carriage shall return and either bring him also, or send him on to his father's. Though I am almost afraid to do this, for fear of alarming the good old colonel and his wife,' said General Fielden, gently.

Immediately after this brief conference, preparations were made to remove Mr. Wyndham and Blanche. With a little support, they were now sufficiently revived to walk to the carriage, which they would not do till they had spoken a few words of grateful solicitude to Captain Haverty, who was now able, with a little help from Patrick O'Brien, to sit up and return their earnest congratulations.

'We are going to take Mr. Wyndham and his daughter to my house, William,' said General Fielden; 'and, if you like, my carriage shall come back and bring you too. The doctor wishes you to remain here a little longer before you are disturbed by removal; but if you will allow me, I shall only be too happy to have you in my house also.'

'No, I thank you, general; I feel much better already, and I dare say I shall be able to walk home shortly, where I should like to be before my mother hears anything of either the fire or my slight injuries.'

29—2

'Well, you shall have my carriage home, at all events,' rejoined the general, who appreciated his affectionate solicitude for his mother too much to attempt to dissuade him from his wish. 'It will be back quite as soon as it will be advisable for you to move, and I insist upon your not attempting to walk home. — And how are you, my brave fellow?' asked the general, addressing Patrick O'Brien, with a kind look. 'I hope you have not received much injury.'

'Och, yer worship, not a bit, barrin' a scratch or two, an' a few burns,' replied Patrick, looking up cheerfully, in spite of his scratched face, burned hands, and bruised body.

'You're a noble fellow, and shall have your full share of the reward I offered for the rescue of my friends.'

At this moment Colonel Haverty's voice was heard, at the partially closed door, above the hum of the people outside. The general hastily turned round to meet him.

'Good God, general!' exclaimed the colonel, as he entered the coach-house, 'how did this dreadful affair occur? Where are the Wyndhams? Have they all escaped?'

'Yes, thank God! they are all safe, though

they have had a narrow escape. Here they are,' said the general; the Wyndhams at the same moment approaching, with the motive of screening his son from his sight, as much as to receive the colonel's congratulations. 'Our old friend Wyndham and his dear daughter have indeed had a narrow escape,' added the general.

'Thanks be to Almighty God for preserving them!' exclaimed the colonel with hearty earnestness, as he shook Mrs. Wyndham and her husband and their daughter warmly by the hand. 'I am so thankful to see you after the frightful dangers you have been in; I sincerely hope and trust you are not seriously injured in any way.'

'No, I am thankful to say I don't think either myself or my daughter have received any permanent injury; only a little shaken by our recent dangers. Though but for the timely aid and noble services of——' 'your son,' Mr. Wyndham was going to say, but at a glance from the general, he suddenly stopped.

'As soon as I got up, and had ascertained where the fire was, I hastened to offer you my services and the use of my house; and was told my son was here also,' said the colonel, addressing the Wyndhams.

'We are deeply grateful to you for your kindness; but we are just going to General Fielden's,' replied Mr. Wyndham, with some slight embarrassment in his look, as if scarce knowing what to say to the colonel about his son.

'Yes, William is here too,' said General Fielden, trying to conceal his uneasiness.

'Where is he? He hasn't been in any danger, I hope?' exclaimed the colonel, anxiously, suspecting that all was not right with his son.

'He is in none now, at all events,' returned the general. 'In his noble and successful efforts to rescue Mr. Wyndham and his daughter from impending death, he not only encountered great peril, but met with some mishaps. The doctor, however, who fortunately arrived soon after, says there is no occasion for uneasiness. Here is your gallant son,' said he, stepping from before the colonel, who instantly rushed forward and clasped his son's hand in his, exclaiming, in agitated emotion:

'Good heaven, William! what is the matter? Are you hurt?'

'Not much, father; only a little scorched by the fire; and I felt a little faint from the heat and want of air. But I am getting all right now.'

'The Almighty be praised! But why did you, my dear boy, imperil your own life so?' the colonel said, in a tone of anxiety.

'For shame, Haverty,' said General Fielden, good-humouredly, 'to chide your son for only doing what you would have done yourself had you been here, old as you are!'

'You're right, colonel,' replied the other quickly; 'and I cannot blame him for having exposed himself to danger when it was to save the life of a fellow-creature, much less so when it was for our good friend here and his lovely daughter. Thank God that his efforts were successful!'

'I do indeed thank God! and your son too, colonel,' said Mrs. Wyndham, gratefully.

'I have just told your son that after my carriage, which is now here, has conveyed our friends to my house, it shall return and take him home. You will, of course, stay for it?'

'Thank you; I suppose it would not be advisable for him to attempt to walk.'

'I think not, sir,' said the surgeon, who

was standing beside him. 'Captain Haverty is in no danger, but it is necessary not to fatigue or excite him in any way at present.'

Just as Blanche Wyndham had bid William Haverty a silent but tender farewell, and her father and mother, with General Fielden, had done the same, and were preparing to enter the carriage, Mr. James Murray, who had been moving about rather uneasily, sometimes in the coach-house, sometimes among the crowd outside, as if he would gladly have taken his departure, but was either ashamed to do so, or lingered there in hope of saying something congratulatory to the Wyndhams on their escape, or expressive of sympathy for their sufferings, came forward and began to address her as she was led towards the carriage between the general and her mother, followed by her father; but, without even looking at him, she turned her head away, with a feeling of the most inexpressible scorn and disgust. Apparently, however, unabashed, he would still have persisted, had not General Fielden very courteously, but also very distinctly, said:

'Pray, Mr. Murray, do not interrupt us now. Miss Wyndham, as you are aware, is not in a condition, at present, to make it advisable for her to linger in the night air.'

'I only wished to offer my congratulations and to express my pleasure at seeing her out of danger, and so much recovered from the effects of her recent alarming position,' said that gentleman, in a slightly mortified tone, stepping aside to let them pass to the carriage.

'It is very considerate of you, Mr. Murray, to take such an interest in my daughter—now she is safe, and for which we are, of course, greatly indebted to your exertions and services,' returned Mrs. Wyndham, in a tone of calm, ironical respect.

'Well, I do not profess to have made so much show of my feelings and exertions as some others may have done, but no one felt more anxious about the safety of both Mr. Wyndham and Blanche than I did. In fact, if I had felt less anxious I should, I dare say, have been more composed, and——'

'Less alarmed, I suppose,' suggested the lady, with a quiet sneer, as she took her seat in the carriage beside her daughter, who had already been handed in.

'Yes; how could I be otherwise than alarmed to know they were in such dreadful danger?' replied Mr. Murray, apparently resolved not to take offence at the tone of Mrs. Wyndham. 'Good-night, Mr. Wyndham,' said he, taking him by the hand as he was about to step into the carriage after his wife and daughter, the general being behind him. 'I hope I shall be allowed the privilege of calling to see how you are to-morrow?'

'I really cannot venture upon asking any one to see us without General Fielden's invitation, Mr. Murray,' returned Mr. Wyndham, quietly.

'Of course, if Mr. Murray wishes to call to see you, he has just as much liberty to do so at my house, as if it were your own,' said the general, closing the door as Mr. Wyndham took his seat in the carriage, who, turning round, asked him if he were not coming in also.

'No, thank you. I shall go outside with the coachman, and see that he doesn't drive you into any further danger,' replied General Fielden; and turning to Eliza Fleming, who he recognised close to the carriage, desired her to find out the rest of the servants belonging to Mr. Wyndham and bring them with her to his house, after which he immediately drove gently away, having, in the meantime, secured a box of family papers and other documents which had been brought from the house at the commencement of the fire, and taken it, for the greater safety, with himself.

CHAPTER X.

As soon as the carriage had conveyed the Wyndhams to General Fielden's, it was sent back to Bilford Hall, to take home William Haverty and his father. The former was now so much revived that, but for the wishes of the latter, and the opinion of the doctor—who was still with him — he would have declined it, and walked instead of making use of it, even after it arrived; his chief reason for wishing to decline it being his anxiety to avoid alarming his mother. This the colonel was as solicitous about as he was, and decided upon preventing it by stopping the carriage a little before they reached the gate, and walking up to the house.

During their drive, William Haverty briefly related to his father the account of the fire, the fearfully dangerous position in which he had found Mr. Wyndham and Blanche, and the great courage Patrick O'Brien had displayed in so ably assisting him to rescue them from the dreadful death which, but for his timely arrival and aid, in all human probability would have been theirs.

In a few minutes they arrived within a hundred yards of their own gate, where Colonel Haverty and his son, after giving the coachman half-a-crown for himself, left the carriage and walked on towards the house, followed by Patrick, who had come outside with the driver. The surgeon had accompanied them in the carriage and parted from them where they got out, promising to call and see Captain Haverty the next morning.

Mrs. Haverty, who had been very uneasy lest her son had fallen into any danger at the fire, was much relieved when she heard him and her husband again enter the house. She had dressed herself and come downstairs, and was sitting before the fire in the dining-room, which she had made up a little, when they came into the hall. In a moment she was on her feet, opened the room door, and had asked them first about themselves, and then about the fire; nor did her motherly eyes fail in quickly discovering the scorched and singed appearance of her son, as well as a slight degree of pallid tremulousness still in his countenance.

Neither William nor his father had any intention of saying anything about either the danger he had been in, or the important service he had performed for Blanche Wyndham and her father, till the next morning; but they found that this only increased her anxiety and uneasiness, and excited her fears both on account of her son and the Wyndhams. The colonel, therefore, briefly related to her the account he had received of both the fire and her son's gallantry; nor did he forget to give Patrick O'Brien his due share of the praise that he was so well entitled to.

Mrs. Haverty listened to her husband's graphic description of the fire, and her son's dangers and gallant conduct, with mingled feelings of terror, motherly pride, and deep gratitude to Him who had preserved him amid such awful perils, and not only brought him safe out of them, but had enabled him to be the means of saving the lives of others; asking him many an anxious question if he was sure he had not received any injury, and did not feel any pain, as she applied some

cold cream to the burns on his hands and
the scars upon his face—to all of which he
replied with a cheerfulness that speedily dispelled all uneasiness from her mind on these
points. Nor, anxious though he was to
allay his mother's fears, was his cheerfulness
altogether assumed. The consciousness that
he had performed so important a service to
Blanche Wyndham and her father, not only
inspired him with that deep satisfaction
which a generous action always produces in
the mind of him who does it, but with
renewed hope and confidence in his own
fortune: and made him forget in the joyous
anticipation of returning happiness, not only
his past sufferings, but his present pains and
bodily exhaustion.

After a few minutes' cheerful conversation,
exchanging an affectionate good-night with
his parents, William again retired to his own
room, and went to bed; but not before he
had knelt and offered up his most deep,
heart-felt gratitude to Him who had preserved him amid his recent dangers, and
brought him safely out of them all, and enabled him to be the means, in His provi-
dence, of saving the life of one so dear to
him, and her father also; praying earnestly

that they, as well as himself, might in future be protected from all dangers, either to body or soul; and that this late occurrence might be the means of re-establishing that footing of confidence and affection between himself and Blanche Wyndham which had once been theirs, and which he felt was so necessary to his happiness, and believed so requisite for hers also.

It was long before he slept. The agitation and excitement of the last two hours were still too strong within him, to allow the soft wings of slumber to settle upon his busy thoughts and heated imagination. Accustomed as he had been to face the most appalling dangers of the battlefield with comparative indifference, and a sharer he had been in the deadly strife of the most bloody sieges the world had ever seen, without a single sensation of shrinking or fear, William Haverty could not look back upon the dreadful conflagration he had just witnessed, and the awful perils which had surrounded Blanche and her father, and through which he had passed to rescue them, without a slight feeling of horror every now and then shaking his nervous system, such as no other dangers had ever done before.

Next morning, however, he got up not only nothing the worse, but in much better spirits than he had been in for some time. He felt that he had performed an act which not only entitled him to the lasting gratitude of both Blanche Wyndham and her parents, but which also proved the sincerity of his devotion to her, though he would have done just the same for anyone else in the same or similar position of danger, nor ever once have thought that he was doing anything that merited any special notice or extraordinary reward. But when he thought of the means this had afforded him of not only renewing his intercourse with the Wyndhams, but of giving him a claim upon their gratitude and Blanche's affection, which he felt sure they would not be slow to acknowledge, though he would have repelled alike the parents' acquiescence and the daughter's affection, if he had for one moment supposed they were given him out of mere gratitude, or as a reward purchased by his services to them.

But he felt that what he had done had only removed some obstacle, and replaced him upon a position of confidence with regard to Blanche Wyndham and her parents; while the fire of the previous night had also shown the character of his rival in such a light that neither the parents nor their daughter could in the future look upon him with anything like either respect or approval. As for himself, if it had been possible to increase the contempt he already entertained for James Murray, the events of the previous night would have done so. But that was hardly possible; for he had already formed so mean an estimate of both the personal and moral qualities of that gentleman, that no new display of either cowardice or vice could greatly surprise or disappoint him.

William Haverty's chief satisfaction was that he felt his opinion and sentiments toward Mr. James Murray must be, more or less, shared by the father and mother of Blanche Wyndham : and that their indignation and scorn at his cowardly fears in rushing out of the house—as he heard on the previous night—when the fire broke out, and never once venturing to offer any assistance to either Mr. or Mrs. Wyndham or their daughter, when he might have done so, and saved the latter and her father from the dangerous position in which they were afterward placed, without any risk whatever to either himself or them, must be such as would henceforth completely place him beyond the pale of their consideration or respect.

Soon after breakfast, when the surgeon had paid his promised visit, William Haverty went to General Fielden's to inquire for the Wyndhams, and arrived there just as the general was mounting his horse to ride over to call on him. Great was the gallant old soldier's pleasure to find his young friend so little the worse for his recent dangers.

'I'm delighted to see you,' said the general, in a tone of hearty gladness, as he shook him warmly by the hand. 'And you don't feel any bad effects from last night's exertions, I hope?'

'No, general—none whatever. How are Miss Wyndham and her father?'

'I am glad to hear it: though I read that in your look the moment I saw you. And as for Miss Wyndham, she seems, like yourself, nothing the worse for what she underwent: and is in capital spirits—better than I have seen her in for a long time. Nor does her father appear to be so much grieved at the loss and destruction of their house, as he is thankful for the escape they themselves have had from a frightful and untimely death. Mr. Wyndham, I fear, still feels the effects of his fall from the ladder; and I dare say the loss he has sustained vexes him a good deal, as he tells me the house and furniture were not insured.'

'I am sorry to hear they were not. The loss must be very great.'

'Yes, it must indeed. Three thousand pounds will not cover it. That, however, won't hurt him very much, I should think. I only hope he hasn't received any injury of which he does not wish anyone to know.'

'I hope not. You don't apprehend he has, do you?' said William, anxiously.

'Well, I confess I am somewhat afraid he has. I have seen him once or twice, when he thought no one noticed him, put his hand to his side as if in pain: and he looks both pale and uneasy, though he will not own to anything being the matter with him.'

'Has the doctor been here this morning?'

'Yes, but unfortunately I did not see him to ask what he thought. I believe he is coming again in the evening, when I shall make a point of getting his opinion.'

'I hope there is not anything really serious the matter with Mr. Wyndham; though 1 have no doubt the fall to the ground, when the ladder broke, shook him a good deal. I am glad Mrs. Wyndham bears her anxieties so well, and still more so that Blanche does not appear to be any the worse for her late danger.'

'Why, it seems to have done her good, as well as yourself,' replied the general, with a smile. 'But what an unmitigated coward that Murray is!' he added, with a look of scornful indignation. 'I understand if he had made any exertion when the fire was first discovered, he might have saved both Mr. Wyndham and Blanche from the perils to which they were afterwards exposed. But he was so terror-stricken that he rushed out of the house, leaving Mr. Wyndham to get out his wife and daughter as best he could, and seemed perfectly paralysed with fear for his own safety when there was not the slightest risk.'

'I saw him outside when I arrived, but felt too much contempt for him to speak to him,' replied William.

'I felt I could take that riding-whip out of his hand and lay it across his cowardly shoulders,' returned the general, ' when I saw how the fellow was running about, increasing both Mrs. Wyndham's fears and the confusion of the people about the house. One thing, I should hardly think he can have the meanness to show himself to the Wyndhams again after his last night's display.'

'I believe he has meanness enough for anything.'

'Then I hope Mr. Wyndham will have spirit enough to order him to the door if he calls to see them. And as for allowing him to marry Blanche now, after such conduct, I would rather see her marry your man, Patrick!'

'Well, Patrick has this advantage over the craven Murray, at all events,' replied William, smiling—'he has the heart and nature of a gentleman, if not the position of one; and the other has only those of a rude clown, in spite of his position: and Patrick has the fidelity and courage, too, of a brave, generous spirit, while Murray has only the despicable soul of a low, selfish coward. If it hadn't been for Patrick's opportune assistance, I doubt much if I should have been able to save either Blanche or her father, or myself.'

'I doubt if you would, and I shall see that he is not unrewarded for it. As for yourself,' said the general, smiling, 'I think I can tell what your reward is likely to be, so we must not allow him to be without his share also.'

'I shall take care of that,' replied William, slightly blushing; 'though Patrick is not a man to look for any other reward than approbation of his services for what he has done.'

'But come, I dare say you would like to see the Wyndhams, and I know they want to see you. I'll show you in.'

'If it is not too early, I should like to see them,' he replied, with a mingled feeling of happiness and anxiety.

'No, they are ready to see you. They thought that your father—as they did not expect you would be able to call—would most likely come to inquire for them; and wished to see him if he did,' said the general, leading the way into the house, followed by Captain Haverty.

CHAPTER XI.

When General Fielden and William Haverty entered the room where the Wyndhams were, they found Mr. Wyndham lying back in an easy-chair, Blanche half reclining upon a sofa, and Mrs. Wyndham sitting at a small table near them, with an open book before her, from which she had been reading, having just stopped as they opened the door. That book was the Bible. The expression of calm peaceful attention with which her hearers had been listening to her gentle, earnest voice was still upon their faces, and fell impressively upon the hearts of their host and William Haverty, who paused for an instant after opening the door, unwilling to trouble them.

'I am afraid we have disturbed you, Mrs. Wyndham,' said her host apologetically, as if about to retire.

'No, you have not, general,' replied Mrs. Wyndham. 'Come in: I had just finished.'

'Here's a friend come to see you,' said the general, stepping into the room, followed by William Haverty; all the three, at the same moment, starting to their feet in joyful surprise at seeing him.

'William Haverty!' exclaimed Mrs. Wyndham, using her old familiar expression towards him, seizing his hand and almost weeping with mingled feelings of gratitude and gladness; 'I am so glad to see you! We have been so anxious about you; though when the surgeon called a short time ago, he told us you were almost well again, and we were so happy to hear it. How can we ever repay you for the dangers you encountered, and your noble conduct toward my dear husband and our child?'

'The pleasure I now have in seeing you all safe and so well, after your recent perils, are far more than sufficient reward for the services I was fortunate enough to be able to render you,' said William, first glancing at Mrs. Wyndham and her husband, and then at Blanche, warmly shaking hands with them. 'I hope you do not feel any bad effects from your fall,' he continued, addressing Mr.

Wyndham, observing a slight pallor on his face.

'No, not much, at any rate—only a slight pain in my side; but I dare say it is nothing,' said Mr. Wyndham, somewhat uneasily. 'But oh, William !' he added earnestly, 'if it hadn't been for you, and that noble fellow who helped you, where would my dear child and I have been at this moment? We should have been burned to ashes beneath the smouldering ruins of our own house !'

'Oh, I hope not, Mr. Wyndham,' replied William, cheerfully, seeing his painfully agitated manner. 'I hope, if we had not been there to help you, some other persons would; and I am only happy that it fell to my share to be of such service to you in a moment of such extreme danger.'

'Ay! and had one, who I should have expected assistance from, shown even the slightest degree of courage or a desire to help us, when the fire was first ascertained, neither my daughter nor myself would have been exposed to the awful fate from which you rescued us. But, thank God ! we are not beholden to such a despicable fellow for our lives !'

William Haverty was by no means displeased to see the strong feeling of aversion and contempt which Mr. Wyndham now entertained for James Murray, though he made no reply to its expression.

But how can we describe the emotions of Blanche as she met William after the awful dangers they had shared together, and the heroic proof he had given of his unchangeable and devoted love to herself? For some moments she could not speak; but, after pressing his hand for an instant in silence, she sat down upon the sofa and looked up into his face with an expression of the deepest gratitude, half-embarrassed affection, and tender confidence; while he felt scarcely less embarrassed with happiness than she did. And well did that moment's ecstasy of emotion repay him for not only his recent dangers, but all the past doubt and unhappiness he had endured on her account; and had they been ten times more, he would have deemed them as nothing in comparison with the unspeakable felicity he now experienced. It wanted no words to tell him of the full approbation of her parents that he now had to his suit, any more than it did to assure him of her unchanged affection towards himself. There is a deep, mysterious sympathy between the unspoken love of two devoted hearts that no language can give utterance to, and wants no words to be understood between themselves. A look, or a tone of the voice, or a touch of the hand, will often convey far more than the most passionate words could do. And such was now the case with William Haverty and Blanche Wyndham. Each fully understood the thoughts of the other, and seemed to feel that, from henceforth, nothing could ever again occur to interrupt the current of their affection or interpose between them and happiness.

'Oh, William! I am so pleased to see you so little injured after your frightful dangers and exertions to save dear papa and myself last night,' said Blanche, fervidly, being the first to find the use of her tongue.

'Not more so than I am to see you looking so well after what you suffered from the fire and the narrow escape you had.'

'Who was that brave fellow that helped you to get papa down the ladder? General Fielden says he is your servant. Is he really so?'

'Yes; and a braver or more faithful follower no man ever had. He has twice or thrice saved my life, and each time, too, with the most perfect composure and apparent coolness, as if he thought it only his ordinary duty to do so, and the most common occurrence to risk his own life for his master's,' replied Captain Haverty, who felt almost as proud of his servant as his servant did of him.

'What an invaluable servant he must be to you!' said Blanche, warmly.

'He is indeed. I would not lose him for the world.'

'Papa is so grateful to him, too. I hope he will call and allow us to thank him for his great services to us, as well as to enable us to give him a substantial token of our gratitude.'

'If your papa wishes to see him, I can send him; but I doubt if he will get him to accept any payment for doing what was nothing more than his duty, in assisting me to rescue you and your papa from your danger. Besides, I don't altogether like the idea of giving rewards for every generous or brave action a man does.'

'Still, I think he ought to receive some reward from us for what he did; and I am sure papa will not be satisfied if he does not.'

'Of course, William Haverty does not expect any reward for his own services,' said

General Fielden, with a sly smile of good-humour, glancing at Blanche as she spoke, who blushed deeply as she met the rather embarrassed glance of her preserver at this moment fixed upon her. 'Still, that is no reason why his man should not receive the reward his courage and achievements have earned.'

'He's a noble fellow, general, isn't he?' said Mr. Wyndham, warmly. 'I shall take care that he has some befitting recompense for his great services. Next to William Haverty, I feel that I owe my life to the timely and gallant aid of that man, but for whom both I and my poor daughter must have perished in the flames.'

'Well, it was a narrow escape for you both, I confess,' replied General Fielden. 'You have no idea how the fire originated, I suppose?'

'No, none whatever. It commenced, I believe, in the lower part of the house; but where, or how, I cannot tell. No one but ourselves has suffered anything by it, I hope?'

'No; my coachman made inquiries again when he went back last night, after we left, and he could hear of no accident to anyone else.'

'I was so glad to find that all the servants made their escape out of the house so soon after the fire broke out,' remarked Mrs. Wyndham. 'I suppose everything in the house was destroyed?'

'I've not heard anything this morning about it; but I believe almost everything was burned,' replied the general, 'except the box of papers that I got hold of, the plate, and one or two other things which you got out yourselves when the fire first broke out.'

'Yes, my servant had been there this morning before I started, and brought back the intelligence that now nothing remained but a heap of smoking ruins, blackened walls, and charred window-sashes and door-posts,' said William Haverty. 'I didn't go to see it as I came, but intend doing so as I return.'

'Never mind, Wyndham,' said General Fielden in a cheerful tone of sympathetic kindness, observing the sad expression of that gentleman's face at hearing this. 'The loss is very serious, I know; but what is that in comparison with what it would have been, if you and your daughter had perished too?'

'Ay, general, you're right. But still, I cannot think of the destruction of that old house, which has been the home of myself and my father and forefathers for the last two hundred years, without feeling that one tie which bound me to life has been severed.'

There was a sadness in Mr. Wyndham's tone as he said this that almost alarmed his wife and daughter, and created a very uneasy feeling in both the general and William Haverty.

'Wyndham, my friend, you must not talk in that way,' cried his host, rallying him, while Mrs. Wyndham glanced anxiously in the face of her husband, suspecting that it was not right with him, although he would not acknowledge to anything being wrong, or that he was in any pain.

'Oh, papa!' exclaimed Blanche, going up to his chair and kneeling down before him, and gazing up with an alarmed look of tender affection into his face; while Mrs. Wyndham drew closer to him at the same time, with an uneasy look at this unusual despondency on the part of her husband, feeling sure that the mere loss of his property would never have caused it.

'You need not look so frightened, my dears; I didn't mean to alarm you,' said he with a smile of rather forced cheerfulness, addressing his wife and daughter affectionately. 'It's only the thought of the destruction of the old place that makes me feel a little dispirited. I shall be all right again presently.'

'Well, don't think of it, my dear,' replied his wife, cheeringly. 'You mustn't frighten your poor wife and Blanche by talking in that way, or we shall think there's something more the matter with you than you say there is. Are you quite sure, now, you do not feel any pain anywhere?' she inquired, with a rather sudden and anxious look, observing something like an expression of pain in her husband's face.

'No; only a slight twinge in the right side which I fell upon, when the ladder gave way. But it's nothing, I daresay.'

'You didn't fall upon the ladder, did you?' inquired the general, half anxiously.

'I hardly know how I fell. I believe when I came to the ground the man that brought me out of the room was under me. But, as I was falling, I felt something strike me rather sharply on the side, perhaps part of the broken ladder; but I daresay it's only a slight bruise, not worth speaking of.'

'You did not mention it to the surgeon

when he was here, did you?' again inquired the general.

'No, I didn't feel it then. But never mind; I've no doubt but it's only a slight bruise, and will be all right again by to-morrow,' said Mr. Wyndham, making an effort to appear free from pain, though every moment he felt it rapidly increasing.

'I hope it will,' rejoined General Fielden cheerfully, exchanging a glance of some uneasiness with Captain Haverty. 'At all events, when the surgeon comes again this afternoon, you must tell him about it, and get him to give you something, in case of its being troublesome to you.'

'Your man was nothing the worse for his fall, with my weight upon him, I understand, captain,' said Mr. Wyndham, with a smile.

'No, nothing whatever. He seems to possess as many lives as a cat, and generally by some means or other is fortunate enough to escape from all danger without much damage.'

'Now, William,' interposed the general, 'we must not tire our patients out with too much talking. If you're going back now, I'll go as far as Bilford Hall with you, and have a look at the old place.'

'Yes, I am going back now, and shall be happy to walk with you. I shall call again in the evening if you will permit me, and see how Mr. Wyndham is,' he added, addressing Mr. Wyndham, casting an affectionate glance at Blanche at the same time, whose smile of half-bashful encouragement fell like dew upon his heart.

'We shall indeed be happy to see you, if it will not tire you too much to come back again to-day,' said Mrs. Wyndham, kindly.

'Oh, not at all. I am not so easily tired,' he replied, smiling.

Wishing them good-morning, and expressing a hope that he might find Mr. Wyndham better when he came in the evening, William, followed by the general, left the room, taking the road that led past Bilford Hall.

'I don't exactly like that pain in his side of which Mr. Wyndham complains,' remarked General Fielden, after leaving the house, as they walked on together.

'Nor do I. What a pity he did not name it when the surgeon was with him this morning, for if there is any danger the sooner it is known the better.'

'I suppose he did not feel so much then, or probably thought the pain would go off itself; so did not complain, fearing it might make his wife uneasy.'

'I've a good mind to call on the surgeon before I go home and tell him about it,' said our hero, thoughtfully.

'I think you had better : for I confess I feel rather uneasy.'

'So do I, and will call as I proposed.'

CHAPTER XII.

As Captain Haverty and his friend approached Bilford Hall, they saw several people upon the spot, and some of them scraping among the ruins, evidently in hopes of finding something valuable. Among them was Bilson, from the market-garden on the opposite side of the hill, who was just putting something into his pocket, and slunk away as he saw them.

Mr. Wyndham's gardener and coachman had been sent to keep off strangers, and to prevent anything being carried away; but he was so full of self-important talk about the fire, with two or three persons from the village, that he was paying but little attention to anything else.

'Hollo! what do you want here? What's that you've put in your pocket?' cried the general to Bilson.

'Why nothing,' replied Bilson, with his usual surly down-looking expression of countenance, stopping short.

'Well, you're not wanted here, at all events, so you had better be off,' returned the general.

'I'm just going,' rejoined the man in a half-insolent tone, moving slowly away from the spot.

'There's a thievish look about that fellow that I don't at all like,' remarked General Fielden, as Bilson disappeared round the corner of the lane, and took his way toward the footpath leading in the direction of his own house.

'I do not like him either,' replied Captain Haverty; 'and hope he has not picked up anything of value. I thought there was a guilty look about him when you asked what it was, that made me rather suspicious.'

'Well, if I thought he really had found anything valuable I would have him brought back yet;' but Bilson was already some distance off, ascending the side of the hill, where, for a short time, he was visible from where they stood. 'Confound the fellow! that haste of his does certainly look rather suspicious after all. But he is too far gone now, I'm afraid, to call him back.'

'Perhaps it's only some trifling thing not worth troubling about,' returned William Haverty. 'I believe very little was saved except the plate and some family papers, which were fortunately got out before the fire reached them.'

'Yes, the plate and family papers were saved and taken to my house; and they were almost the only things of value that were saved, I believe. But here comes Mr. James Murray,' the general added, as that gentleman rode up to the gate upon his grey horse, where he stopped for a few seconds, looking towards the ruins, and then, probably seeing the general and Captain Haverty, and not wishing to encounter them, rode on in the direction of the general's residence.

'He's off to call upon the Wyndhams, I suppose,' continued the general. 'After his cowardly conduct last night, I wonder he is not ashamed to appear before them.'

'I don't think there is much more sense of shame than there is of honour in him,' replied William, with a sneer.

'I don't think there is; although he was evidently ashamed to come up and meet us here just now,' smiled the general.

'Or, probably, he may prefer seeing the Wyndhams while you are not there to witness the interview.'

'Well, I'm greatly mistaken if he will be very anxious to make a second call upon them in a hurry. One good result of the fire, at all events, will be that it has destroyed for ever, I should think, all his pretensions to the hand of Blanche Wyndham, and restored some one else to the position he so much longed for—and which is so agreeable to the young lady herself, too,' he added with a smile.

'I'm glad you think so, general,' replied William, slightly blushing, but trying to look as if he did not feel that any of the remarks applied to himself.

'As I am thus far, I think I shall walk on with you, and call upon your father and mother, and see how they are,' said General Fielden, after they had walked about among the ruins of the house for a few minutes.

'I shall be very glad, and so will they, I am sure. Only before I go in, I must walk on and see if Mr. Rance, the surgeon, is at home, and tell him about Mr. Wyndham, and ask him to call upon him as soon as he can, in case there should be anything serious the matter with his side.'

This William Haverty accordingly did.

In the meantime Mr. James Murray, glad to think he was not likely to encounter General Fielden, rode on to call upon the Wyndhams. The moment it was announced to them that Mr. Murray was at the door, and would be glad to see them, Blanche hastened from the room, and did not return while he remained.

'How d'ye do, Mrs. Wyndham? I am glad to see you after your last night's alarm!' exclaimed Mr. Murray, as he entered, in a tone of congratulation and fond earnestness, though evidently uncertain what reception to expect, speaking in his usual rather loud voice of rough pomposity; 'and I am so glad, too, to see Mr. Wyndham after his recent dangers and heavy loss,' he added somewhat uneasily, observing a degree of coolness in the look both of Mr. and Mrs. Wyndham, as he spoke.

'We are obliged to you, Mr. James Murray,' said Mr. Wyndham, drawing himself up in his chair, with a stiff, formal bend of the head to his visitor, without making any offer of his hand, while Mrs. Wyndham slightly bowed also, drawing back as Mr. Murray approached to shake hands with her; 'and also,' continued Mr. Wyndham, 'for the help and assistance we had from you.'

'My efforts, I confess, were not so useful to you as they might have been,' returned Mr. Murray, somewhat confused, but with a look of forced composure; 'but my anxiety on account of the danger you and Blanche were in, made me so agitated that I did not know what to do.'

'I suppose it did, Mr. Murray,' returned Mr. Wyndham, drily.

'How is Blanche? I hope she has recovered from the effects of her danger,' said Mr. Murray, turning to Mrs. Wyndham with increased uneasiness.

'My daughter is as well as we can expect; in fact, better in some respects than she has been for a long time,' returned Mrs. Wyndham, composedly.

'I am glad to hear it—I am so glad to hear it, as I was afraid she might feel the effects of her alarming danger so much more than even you or Mr. Wyndham.'

'No; I am happy to say that the danger she was in last night, from the fire, has not affected her nearly so much as a danger of another kind, of which this has now relieved her,' returned Mrs. Wyndham, with a glance of something like contempt.

'Indeed! I didn't know she had been in any danger from anything else,' said Mr. Murray, scarcely knowing what to think of Mrs. Wyndham's remark and manner. 'I suppose I shall have the pleasure of seeing her presently,' he added after a moment's pause.

'I doubt if it would be any pleasure to her, Mr. Murray, whatever it might be to you,' said Mr. Wyndham coldly, slightly pressing his right side as he spoke.

'Indeed, Mr. Wyndham! What do you mean? How am I to understand this—this extraordinary reception? Am I now to suppose that, after all the attention I have paid your daughter, and in spite of our approaching marriage, you wish to treat me with disrespect?'

'It is no disrespect to any man to treat him as he deserves to be treated, sir,' replied Mr. Wyndham, his pale cheeks becoming slightly flushed. 'Your conduct last night, Mr. Murray, has opened my eyes to the grievous injustice of which I have been guilty in trying to force my daughter to marry a man she disliked; for you are well enough aware she never expressed anything but aversion to you. But, thank God! it is not too late for her happiness and my own peace of mind, even now,' he added fervently.

'Am I to suppose, Mr. Wyndham, that after all the expense I have been at with my house and furniture, and the preparations I have been making for our marriage, you wish to break off your daughter's engagement with me ?' asked Mr. Murray, in a rude tone.

'Yes; such is both my wish and determination.'

'Surely, Mrs. Wyndham, your husband is either labouring under some extraordinary excitement of feeling, or some one who I know has long endeavoured to create a prejudice in your mind against me, for the furtherance of his own deceitful objects, has made him forgetful of not only what is due to me as a gentleman, but as the future husband of your daughter,' said Mr. Murray, turning to Mrs. Wyndham.

'I believe, Mr. Murray,' replied the lady, in a calm, measured tone, that my husband is neither labouring under any excitement, nor has been prejudiced against you by anyone else, as you insinuate. In fact, I consider such an insinuation against the gentleman to whose courage we are indebted for the life of our child, as well as my husband, little less than an insult. You ought to know us better than to think we would listen to anything about you from another, even if you are so ignorant of the character of Captain Haverty, or of any gentleman, in short, as to suppose he would do anything of the kind. He has never even mentioned your name to us. And as for your ever being the husband of my daughter, that you shall never be with my consent, nor yet, I think, with my husband's. And, of course, you know well enough she has never had any desire for it herself, but, on the contrary, always expressed the greatest aversion to you.'

'Then, madam, why wasn't this told me before?' asked Mr. Murray, angrily.

'You knew it perfectly well. The match was never one that I either approved of or liked; and it was only because Mr. Wyndham approved of it that I consented at all, and, very much against both my own feelings and my daughter's, agreed to your proposals. But, what with the dreadful dangers we have escaped, and the conduct you exhibited last night, we have resolved at once to break off all further intercourse with you, either upon this subject or any other.'

'What!' exclaimed the disappointed suitor; 'am I to be subject to such treatment from such as you? I will expose you over the whole of the county.'

'You are perfectly welcome to do that, if you like,' said Mrs. Wyndham, quietly; 'though I'm afraid it would only be exposing yourself much more than us. I do not imagine you would gain very much of either credit or sympathy for your trouble, Mr. Murray.'

'Mr. Wyndham, do you really mean to act in this way toward me, after all that I have done, and all the sacrifices of station and family I was willing to make to marry your daughter?'

'Sir!' said Mr. Wyndham, with an indignant look, 'such insolent arrogance only the more strongly convinces me of your contemptible meanness, rudeness, to say nothing of your want of principle. How dare you talk so of either my daughter or myself! You make sacrifices, indeed, to marry her! The blood of the Wyndhams is as good as that of the Murrays ever was, or ever will be; aye, a thousand times better, or I'm mistaken; it never yet was known to circulate in the veins of either a knave or a coward, which is more than can be said of theirs, now at any rate!'

'Come, dear Wyndham, do not allow him to vex you. You know you are not able to stand any excitement yet,' said Mrs. Wyndham, with affection, anxiously trying to soothe the irritation of her husband.

'I feel it, my dear,' replied Mr. Wyndham, almost fainting; 'but I cannot hear such insulting language without being excited at it. Had he used the same towards me twenty-four hours ago, old man as I am, he should have found to his cost that——'

'Never mind, my dear,' said his wife, interrupting him, and again trying to soothe his excitement. 'Perhaps Mr. Murray will go, and leave me to keep you quiet, as he must see you are not in a state to bear any agitation at present.'

'I must have a positive answer to my question first,' replied that gentleman, evidently quite indifferent to Mr. Wyndham's feelings or pain.

'What question do you allude to, Mr. Murray?' asked the lady.

'Whether it is really your intention to

break off the engagement between me and your daughter,' he replied.

'Mr. Murray,' said Mr. Wyndham, with constrained composure and firmness, 'I have already answered that question; and can only repeat what I have before said. My daughter cannot now become your wife. This trial we have just had has opened our eyes to the cruel injury I was doing her in trying to force her to marry a man she neither loved nor respected, and who has given but too good proofs of his unworthiness of her; and I almost feel as if God had sent this upon me as a punishment for the injustice of which I have been guilty toward my own loving, dutiful child, whose feelings ought to have been more carefully considered in my late endeavours to induce her to enter into an alliance with you, contrary to her wishes.'

'Then, sir, I consider your conduct to me most disgraceful. You have been merely trifling with me, and I will not submit to it!' exclaimed Mr. Murray, fiercely.

As if struck by electricity, Mr. Wyndham started to his feet, with a clenched hand, flashing eye and flushed cheek, but the next moment fell back exhausted into his chair, while his wife seized an eau-de-Cologne bottle, and pouring a little in her hand, rubbed it upon his temples, which had the effect of soon somewhat reviving him.

'Mr. Murray,' said she, with calm, concentrated energy of voice, 'are you not ashamed, when you see the dangerous state my husband is in, to stand there and excite him so? If you do not leave us, I shall ring the bell and desire General Fielden's man to show you out. If the general had been in you dared not have used us so.'

'Am I not to see Blanche, then, before I go?' he inquired, in a more conciliatory, or rather more cowed, tone.

'No, Mr. Murray, you must be aware that my daughter can have no pleasure in seeing you, and if you had any respect for us, or regard for either my own or my husband's feelings, you would not make such a request —especially at such a time as this.'

'Then, I say again, your conduct to me is most disgraceful, and I will not submit to it,' rejoined Mr. Murray, fiercely.

'You can do what you like, Mr. Murray,' said Mrs. Wyndham, contemptuously. 'One thing I am determined you shall do, and that is, you shall leave this room,' she added, pulling the bell-rope. 'Be so good as to show Mr. Murray out,' she added, addressing the footman as he entered, who seemed rather surprised at the tone and look of Mrs. Wyndham as she spoke.

'Yes, ma'am,' replied the servant, holding the door open for Mr. Murray to pass.

'Your master isn't in, is he, Benjamin?' inquired Mr. Murray, addressing the footman, with a flushed face. 'These people have grossly insulted me, and I wish to know if it is with his sanction that they do so in his house.'

'I'm sorry to hear it, sir; but master has given me orders to do whatever Mr. and Mrs. Wyndham wish,' returned the footman quietly, but respectfully.

'Well, then, I shall relieve you of my presence for a time,' said Mr. Murray, turning round to Mr. and Mrs. Wyndham, as he was about to leave the room; 'but General Fielden shall hear of the manner I have been treated, and insulted in his house by you;' and with a fierce scowl, he stalked out of the room, mounted his horse, which he had left at the door in charge of the general's coachman, and rode off in the direction of Westdon, furious with rage and mortification at the result of his visit to the Wyndhams.

'Curse that whelp of an Irishman! He's at the bottom of all this. But I may, perhaps, undermine him yet—at all events I shall have my revenge upon him before many days pass,' he muttered between his clenched teeth. 'Now for Bilson. I shall see what he can do,' he added, spurring his horse into a canter, and was soon out of sight.

CHAPTER XIII.

Fortunately Captain Haverty found the surgeon at home, who promised to call and see Mr. Wyndham in the course of an hour; he arrived at General Fielden's house not long after Mr. James Murray had left. The moment he saw his patient and had examined his side, he seemed to think there was no small amount of danger. He found that two of the ribs on the right side were broken, and had penetrated the lungs, which were already in a very painful and dangerous state of inflammation. The late excitement caused by Mr. Murray had, of course, greatly increased this; and every moment the danger was rapidly advancing.

Without telling Mrs. Wyndham the full extent of her husband's condition, the surgeon said that he had received very serious injury, and that if she had no objection he should like to have the opinion and advice of a physician, in case of any danger; and above all things it was necessary for Mr. Wyndham to be kept perfectly quiet, and free from all excitement and anxiety.

Mrs. Wyndham, of course, agreed to everything that the doctor proposed, and was just about to ring the bell and ask if anyone could be had to go to Westdon to bring back a physician to consult with Mr. West, when General Fielden entered the room.

'Good-morning, Mr. West. How do you find Mr. Wyndham now?' asked the general.

'Humph! not quite so well as I should have liked, general,' he replied, slowly. 'I have just told Mrs. Wyndham I should like to have the opinion of a physician, and she was just going to ring the bell to see if one of your servants would go into the town and bring back Sir Henry Smith.'

'Do you think there is any danger, then?' inquired the general, uneasily.

'Well, there might be,' returned Mr. West, cautiously, avoiding to say anything to excite alarm in either his patient or Mrs. Wyndham. 'It seems that one or two ribs are broken, and unfortunately they have entered the lungs a little, which has caused some degree of inflammation, as well as internal hemorrhage, which I must endeavour to allay and stop. There is also some strong excitement upon him, which I must try to keep down, if possible.'

'Do you feel in much pain, Mr. Wyndham?' asked the general, gently laying his hand upon his arm.

'No, not very much: only at times,' replied the other.

'That's good: we shall soon put you all right, I daresay,' rejoined the general, cheeringly. 'I suppose you are willing to have Sir Henry Smith sent for?'

'Yes, if Mr. West wishes it.'

'I should rather have his opinion, in case of the affair taking a worse turn than we expect,' replied the surgeon.

'Oh yes, general; by all means let us have a physician,' said Mrs. Wyndham, anxiously.

'Then I will send off my coachman for him at once,' replied General Fielden, leaving the room; Mr. West, without any apparent uneasiness, following him.

'Will you kindly desire your man to make as much haste as he can,' said the surgeon in an undertone, as they reached the hall.

'Do you think there is any immediate danger?'

'I fear there is. If Mr. Wyndham had told me of this in the morning, I might perhaps have been able to counteract the inflammation before it gained so much hold upon his lungs, and prevented the hemorrhage, too, which seems to me to have only recently commenced to any serious extent; but his not saying anything of it then, has considerably increased both his own danger and my difficulty in treating him. And, if I might venture to do so, I should propose, if it would not take much time to get it ready, that you send your own carriage to bring Sir Henry Smith, which will all the more facilitate his coming.'

'Thank you for reminding me; I shall do so. But suppose Sir Henry is not at home?'

'He is almost sure to be at home, if your man gets to his house quickly. He seldom goes out before two o'clock; and if he should be, they will know where to find him.'

'Harvey,' said the general, addressing his coachman, who had already been summoned, as he made his appearance, 'put the bay horse into the light basket-carriage as quick as you can, and drive into the town for Sir Henry Smith, to see Mr. Wyndham, as fast as you are able, and bring him back with you. Don't lose a moment if you can help it.'

'Stay: give him my card, immediately. He will know it is important, and come at once,' said the surgeon, writing a couple of words on the card, and giving it to the coachman.

In a few minutes the carriage was on the road for the physician, and Mr. West and the general had again returned to the room where Mr. and Mrs. Wyndham were. Blanche having left the room when the surgeon first came, knowing he was still there, had not returned, though in great anxiety to know his opinion, which was all the more increased by observing the carriage so hastily sent off; the object of which was, she suspected, to procure further advice for her father.

'Mr. Wyndham has not been exerting himself, or excited in any way, has he, since the morning, Mrs. Wyndham?' asked the surgeon, as they returned to the room.

'There has been a gentleman here who has made him rather excited and agitated,' replied Mrs. Wyndham in an undertone, as if unwilling to allude to Mr. Murray's visit in her husband's hearing.

'I thought so, and am sorry for it; I fear it has done Mr. Wyndham very considerable injury,' returned Mr. West, gravely.

'Oh, I was afraid it would,' said Mrs. Wyndham. 'I wish I had said we could not see him.'

'It's Mr. James Murray you allude to, is it not?' asked General Fielden aside, as the doctor turned to his patient, having in the meantime applied some lotion to the bruise on his side and given him something to compose him, as well as to stop the hemorrhage, but which had apparently produced little or no benefit as yet.

'Yes, he has been here, and behaved very rudely; in fact with extreme violence.'

'Indeed! I wish I had been at home,' said the general, indignantly. 'I should have ordered him to the door for his impertinence.'

'Well, I was obliged to do that myself,' rejoined Mrs. Wyndham, in a few words relating what had passed.

'The scoundrel! If I had been in, I

would have horse-whipped him out of the house!' exclaimed the general, flushed with anger; 'and if he calls here again, I shall order him off the premises. Where is Miss Wyndham? He did not see her, I suppose?'

'No; she had left the room before he came in, and had not returned. She went upstairs, I believe, when Mr. West came, and is waiting till he's gone, I suppose, before she comes down again.

At this moment, Blanche, unable to remain in suspense by herself any longer, slowly and most timidly opened the door, and entered the room. With one quick glance she seemed to comprehend both the danger of her father and the anxiety of her mother. Without speaking, she walked softly up to the former: and bending down before him, took up his half-drooping hand and pressed it to her lips with an expression of the deepest reverence and affection.

'God bless you, my dear child!' said the father with earnest emphasis, laying his hand gently upon her head, while a smile passed over his face.

'Blanche, dear,' said Mrs. Wyndham, beckoning her daughter to her, 'don't be alarmed. Your father is very poorly, but we hope there is no immediate danger; only you must not agitate him in any way. We have sent into the town for Sir Henry Smith, who will soon be here, we hope. So don't be frightened, my dear; he will be better soon.'

'Oh, mamma! I know poor papa is so ill —so very ill!' said Blanche, in a deep, earnest whisper of suppressed emotion and affection.

'I know he is very poorly, dear; but we must not let him see that we think so. It will only make him worse, by increasing his anxiety on our account; and Mr. West has just said he must be kept as quiet and undisturbed as possible.

'Oh, I wish Dr. Smith would come!' said Blanche, with intense earnestness, casting an anxious look of affection on the pale countenance of her father, who now, under the effects of the composing medium Mr. West had given him, seemed less uneasy, and apparently half dozing.

'So do I wish Sir Henry Smith would come,' was the equally earnest but unexpressed thought of both Mrs. Wyndham and General Fielden, as they saw the decreasing energies of the invalid.

'How do you think he is now?' inquired

the general, as Mr. West approached the recess of the large bay window where he, with Mrs. Wyndham and Blanche, was standing.

'I don't think he is worse than when I came. I am in hopes that the medicine I gave him has stopped the internal hemorrhage a little, if not wholly; and, as he seems inclined to sleep, perhaps it may do him no harm if he does go off for a few minutes,' replied the doctor.

'Then perhaps we had better leave the room for a time?' suggested the general.

'It would be better if you would do so,' said the surgeon, quietly; 'as the least sound might disturb or startle him, which I wish, if possible, to avoid.'

'Blanche, dear, you had better go with General Fielden. I shall remain with your father,' said Mrs. Wyndham.

'Oh, let me stay too. I won't move.'

'I think you had better not remain, Miss Wyndham,' said Mr. West. 'When Mr. Wyndham wakes up I will send for you, and then you can come in again. But at present, the fewer in the room the better. Won't you go, too, for a few minutes, Mrs. Wyndham?'

'No; I cannot leave my husband until I

see some change for the better, Mr. West. You have no objection for me to remain, I suppose?'

'None whatever, if you prefer it.'

'Well, Blanche, you and I will leave them for a short time,' said the general.

'Now, mamma, you will let me know when papa wakes up, won't you, dear?' said Blanche, with an anxious glance at her father as she turned to leave the room.

'Yes, my dear; and don't be frightened. I hope he'll be better when he wakes.'

'Oh, I do hope so!' fervently whispered Blanche, as she followed General Fielden out of the room.

In the meantime, utterly regardless of the injurious effects of his conduct upon Mr. Wyndham, Mr. James Murray rode on, and arrived at the house of the gardener, Bilson, where he found that worthy just returned from his visit to the ruins of Bilford Hall.

'Well, Tom, I suppose you've been over the hill to see the remains of old Wyndham's place this morning?' said Murray, in a familiar tone, as Bilson came forward as he was fastening his horse to the ring in the wall outside the door of the house, as usual.

'Yes, I have,' replied the other. 'You didn't come that way, I suppose?'

'I rode past it, that was all.'

'I saw General Fielden and that young Irish ——,' remarked Bilson, with a coarse oath, which we prefer omitting.

'Humph! Did you? I wish that young Irish ——, as you call him,' returned Murray, repeating the other's words, 'had been burned and buried beneath those infernal old walls of Wyndham's. And if Fielden had been with him I shouldn't have regretted even that very much,' said he, with a coarse laugh.

'Well, that's very charitable in yee,' said Bilson, with a grin.

'Where's your wife?' demanded Murray, as if half-offended at the sneering tone in which the other made his remark.

'Why, in the house, I suppose,' replied the worthy husband, with a half-sulky nod of his head toward the door. 'But I want to speak to yee afore yee go in.'

'Well, what is it? You don't want any more money to-day, do you?' inquired Murray, with an impatient look.

'No, not 'xactly that,' said Bilson; 'though I hope as how I shall get some money for it!'

'Money for what?' asked Murray, in surprise. 'What do you mean?'

'Why, for something I picked up at Bilston Hall this morning.'

'You're more likely to get sent to the county gaol for it, I expect, if it's found out.'

'That's more than yee dare do, at all events,' retorted Bilson, sulkily. 'But if yee don't want to know what it is, I don't care—only it relates more to yee than yee think, I expect.'

'To me! What is it?' inquired Mr. Murray, eagerly. 'Why didn't you tell me so at first?'

'Yee didn't give me time. But I can't show it to yee here. We must go round by the end of the house, out of sight of the road first,' said Bilson, leading the way, followed by James Murray, who wondered what it could be.

'Here it is,' said Bilson, as soon as they were out of view from the road, taking a largish packet from his pocket, tied with a piece of red tape, and inscribed outside, 'The last Will and Testament of Edward Wyndham, Esquire, of Bilford Hall.'

'Why, this is Mr. Wyndham's will!' exclaimed Mr. Murray. 'How did you get hold of it?'

'I found it this morning among some rubbish, half burned,' said Bilson, 'and put it in my pocket to see what it was.'

'But you didn't think it was of any use to you, did you?'

'Humph! I don't know that. I suppose them as is interested in it won't mind givin' something for it?'

'You had better take care that you don't get yourself into trouble about it,' said Mr. James Murray, somewhat uneasily.

'Oh, there ain't no danger o' that. 'Yee're the only one that knows as I have it; so, if I do get into any trouble, I shall know who's the cause of it.'

'You don't think I am going to get you into trouble, do you?'

'I don't think as how yee will, when yee read this,' replied Bilson, confidently.

'Indeed! Well, as you have opened it, I suppose I may read it—especially as you say it concerns me. You've read it, then?'

'Yes; I read a bit on it after I came home.'

'By heaven! Bilson, if this is all right it will be the best day's work you ever did bringing it to me!' exclaimed Mr. Murray, after running his eye over the will.

'Ay! I thought it would please yee. But I did not bring it to give to yee.'

'Why, what are you going to do with it? It's no use to you.'

'I ain't so sure on that. At all events, I shall keep it and see.'

'You can do as you like; but it's no use to you, nor yet to anybody as yet, for it's only on Wyndham's death that it can be of use to anyone. And he may make another will before that, and then this would be worth nothing.'

'Why, I know that; but suppose he dies now? I hear he is very ill this morning from the effects of the fire. Suppose he was to die now, what would this be worth to me?'

'Nothing, unless his family knew he had made a will, and offered a reward to anyone who could produce it; and then you might get something for it.'

'Well, in that case, what would yee give me for it?'

'I tell you what, Bilson,' said Mr. James Murray, earnestly, seeing it would be no use attempting to deceive him as to the importance of the will; 'if Mr. Wyndham dies now, without making any other will, this will be worth more than thirty thousand pounds to me, if I can carry out what he intends me to do here. If so, you shall have a thousand pounds for your trouble. And here's a five-pound note for you now : only you mustn't let a soul know that you have it ; and for God's sake take care you don't lose it.'

'Oh, I shall keep it safe enough,' replied the fellow, pocketing the note ; ' I've got a secure place to keep it in. Only I must have more than a thousand pounds as my share, mind that !'

' Why, as far as the will is concerned, you couldn't get sixpence for it.'

' Couldn't I ? Don't yee think Mrs. Wyndham would give anything for it ?'

' I can't say. Not much, I'll be bound ; as, if this will is not found, there may be some previous one which is even more favourable to her than this is. It is much more valuable to me than anybody else.'

'Yes ; if yee can get Miss Wyndham to marry yee,' said Bilson, dryly.

' Exactly ; but with such a clear expression of her father's wish as this contains, she would feel bound to do so ; and her mother would think the same. It seems the will was only made about a month ago; so there is not much chance of any other having been made since.'

'But if yee get all this money by it, mind, I must have more than a thousand pounds for my share!' rejoined Bilson, folding up the will and retying it with the tape.

'Well, I may perhaps want to employ you again in some way connected with this affair, and I shall not stint you; if you serve me well I shan't stand upon two or three hundred more, if all goes right. But we must be very still and cautious for a few days till we see how it fares with Wyndham, who is very bad. I saw him this morning, in fact had a few words with him; and he looked to me in a very precarious state. I believe he has injured himself internally in some way. If he dies now, and I should marry his daughter, which, with this to support my suit, I should be sure to do,' said Mr. Murray, with a brightening countenance, quite indifferent to what he knew had occurred to change the wishes and feelings of Mr. Wyndham since the will had been made, 'this will entitles me to ten thousand pounds as a marriage portion with his daughter, and the whole of his estate at his wife's leath; for you saw, I suppose, that he expressly gives to his daughter ten thousand pounds on her marriage with James Murray, esquire, and the whole of his landed estate and other property at the decease of his wife to her also, which is pretty much the same as if he had given it to myself.'

'Yes, I saw that. But suppose she doesn't marry yee? What do you get then?'

'Nothing at all, of course,' replied James Murray, rather impatiently at being so familiarly spoken to and questioned by a man like Bilson.

'Oh, I see; and in case you don't succeed, yee think I may be able to help yee?'

'Perhaps so. But I shall see by-and-by. In the meantime, as I have said, we must keep this matter perfectly quiet. Should I hear anything about a will--that is, if Mr. Wyndham should go off now—or any reward be offered to anyone who produces it, I will let you know.'

'But if they offer any reward for it, and I give it up, what about your promise of the thousand pounds?'

'Oh, that won't interfere with my promise to you: as if Mr. Wyndham does die, it's only after his wife and General Fielden, who

I see are his executors, have got possession of the will, that it becomes of any service to me. And even if they don't offer any reward for its recovery, as they perhaps may not know of its existence, we must see to convey it to them in some way or other; though I dare say Mrs. Wyndham will know something of it, and will cause search to be made for it, and probably offer a reward to anyone who can bring it to her.'

So saying, the would-be husband of Blanche Wyndham left Bilson in the garden and went into the house for a short time; after which he came out, and mounting his horse, rode into Westdon to attend to some magisterial duties at the county hall.

CHAPTER XIV.

Sir Henry Smith soon arrived. After he had seen Mr. Wyndham, and examined his side and asked a few questions of Mr. West, and expressed approval of that gentleman's mode of treatment, he at once said there was no hope of recovery. Mr. West had already formed the same opinion; and a single glance exchanged between them conveyed this to each other.

'Is Mrs. Wyndham at all aware of the danger of her husband?' inquired the physician, in an undertone to Mr. West.

'I scarcely think she is,' returned the surgeon, glancing towards her, as she stood near the window, with General Fielden and her daughter, who had again entered the room, watching every expression of the physician's and surgeon's faces as they talked together for a few minutes, after examining Mr. Wyndham's side, and who was now in rather less pain, and not quite so faint as he had been a short time before.

'Well, I think she had better be made acquainted with it.'

'Will you be so kind as to do it?' asked Mr. West. 'I should be glad if you would.'

'Certainly I will, if you would rather I did it,' said the physician; and addressing Mrs. Wyndham, 'Will you allow me a few minutes' conversation with you in another room, Mrs. Wyndham?' said he, approaching her, and speaking in a low voice. 'Perhaps Miss Wyndham had better remain here with Mr. West and her father. General Fielden can go with us if he likes,' he added, as Mrs. Wyndham, with a slightly quivering lip and sudden pallor in her face, turned with him toward the door, which the general, without any remark, opened, and led them into another room.

'Mrs. Wyndham,' said the physician, in a grave, though kindly, sympathetic voice, 'I think it is only my duty to let you know that your husband is seriously ill'—he seemed almost afraid to come to the point at once.

'Oh, do not say so!' she exclaimed, trembling with fear and emotion.

'I assure you I wish I could conscientiously comply with your request, Mrs. Wyndham; but I should not be speaking honestly if I said anything else.'

'Do you really think Mr. Wyndham is in any immediate danger, Sir Henry?' inquired General Fielden, anxiously.

'Well, I fear he is.'

'O Dr. Smith! Cannot you do anything to save him?' exclaimed Mrs. Wyndham, with agonising earnestness.

'Mr. West has used the very best means of doing so, and to some extent they have had effect; but I fear it will only be temporary: a very short time, however, will decide. But I can hold out little hopes of his recovery; and feel it is only my duty to prepare you for the worst. I trust Mr. Wyndham is prepared for what I fear will too soon be his great change.'

'O my husband! my dear husband!' cried Mrs. Wyndham, with repressed emotion. 'Do not say that I am going to lose him! Oh, do not frighten me by saying so! Tell me he may yet recover! Only say that, and I shall be happy.'

With the true instincts of real sympathy, General Fielden made no effort to interrupt the deep, earnest burst of Mrs. Wyndham's grief; but turned away, too much overcome by her distress to be able to offer any consolation to her. Nor was the physician much less affected.

'God knows, Mrs. Wyndham, how much more gratified I should be to say that! But I feel I should only be deceiving you. I hope you will struggle against your grief, bear your affliction as one who feels that the separation about to take place between you and your beloved husband is not for ever; that one day you will be again united to him, when sorrow, pain, and death are no more. He who died to redeem us will Himself wipe away all tears from our eyes!'

There was a gentle earnestness in the good physician's look, tone, and manner, as he uttered these few solemn words, which deeply impressed and interested his two listeners. They were not the mere formal expressions of commonplace sympathy, but those of a man deeply imbued with the truth of what he said, as well as anxious to soothe the mental anguish of her he spoke to.

'O Dr. Smith!' said Mrs. Wyndham, with

a deep sigh, looking up after a few moments' painful silence ; ' it is very hard—very hard, to part with so good and tender a husband, and be left alone in the world !'

'Do not say alone, my dear Mrs. Wyndham!' said General Fielden, with earnest emotion. 'You have still friends to counsel and cheer you, and an affectionate, amiable daughter to love and comfort you.'

'My poor daughter, too, will be left without a father to direct and watch over her ! O general, when I think of this, it is almost too much for me to bear !' returned Mrs. Wyndham, in a tone of deep, painful emotion.

'While I live, Mrs. Wyndham, neither you nor your daughter shall ever want either a friend or counsellor—or a protector,' rejoined General Fielden, ' if it should be necessary. Nor am I the only one you can count upon in this respect.'

'But there is no one I can rely upon like him.'

'I know it, my dear Mrs. Wyndham,' replied the general, kindly. 'But you must not give way too much.'

'No; I must endeavour to do my duty. Shall we go to my husband again ?' she asked, turning to the physician, and making an effort to appear less agitated, for she was anxious to be again with him.

'Yes, if you feel sufficiently composed to do so,' he replied, quietly opening the door, and leading the way as he spoke, followed by Mrs. Wyndham and the general.

Mr. Wyndham looked up with a faint smile as they entered the room, while Blanche, who was standing beside him, holding his hand, fixed a keen, inquiring glance in their faces, and seemed at once to comprehend the subject and nature of their thoughts.

'You look better, Mr. Wyndham,' said the physician, cheeringly, exchanging a serious glance with Mr. West as he spoke. 'You don't feel quite so much pain now, do you?'

'No, not quite,' he replied, feebly. 'Come, dear wife, you must not look so distressed. It will be all over soon!'

'Don't say that, dearest husband! You will yet be well, I hope,' said Mrs. Wyndham, with repressed emotion, while Blanche raised her handkerchief to her eyes and sobbed aloud.

'Come, dear Blanche!' said her father, gently pulling her toward him, with an affectionate smile, 'you must not grieve your poor father so! I know it is hard for you to lose me, and I feel it is hard—very hard, to leave you and your dear mother; but God's will must be done! It is no use deceiving you with false hopes. I know I cannot live many hours longer. I hope God will take care of you both, and comfort and bless you when I am no longer here to share your cares or your joys with you; and preserve you to Himself, and at last unite us all again, with all dear to us, in His own kingdom, where we shall never, never more be parted!'

He paused, exhausted. There was a slight flush upon his pale face as he said this, which made his hearers hold their breath with awe, and stand as if spell-bound.

'O Edward! It is so sudden! To see you struck down, and taken away from us in this way is very hard to bear!' said Mrs. Wyndham, in a choking voice.

'Yes, my love, it is sudden; but God does everything wisely, and we must submit,' returned the husband, in a resigned voice.

'But do you think there is no hope, Dr. Smith?' asked Mrs. Wyndham, with eager earnestness, turning to that gentleman.

The physician was evidently afraid to trust his voice, and merely slowly shook his head in reply.

'No, no; there is no hope, doctor,' said Mr. Wyndham, who both heard the question and saw the silent answer. 'You know it will soon be all over with me, don't you?'

'I cannot attempt to deceive you, my dear Mr. Wyndham. I fear it will, as far as this world is concerned. All that we can now hope for is that God will sustain you in the last struggles of this life, and give those you leave behind His support also in their sorrowful bereavement.'

'I trust He will, doctor,' said Mr. Wyndham, with a look of hopeful resignation. 'I feel something within me that seems to speak peace to my soul. But I rely not on myself. Oh, that would be poor comfort now! I rely upon One stronger and mightier than man, and whose mercy and love are not less great than His power.'

There was another short silence. Every-one present was too much impressed with the solemnity of the scene, and Mr. Wyndham's words, to be able to speak.

'General,' he continued, after a few moments' pause, 'I hope God will reward you for all this goodness to us; and I am thankful to Him who has given me such a friend in this my last moments.'

'O Wyndham, think not of that; I am only glad to contribute to your ease at such an awful moment. And if there's any request you wish to make—anything you wish me to do for your wife and daughter, do not, I entreat you, hesitate to make it,' replied the general, earnestly, laying his hand upon Mr. Wyndham's as he spoke.

'Thank you. You will take care of my poor wife and child when I am gone, will you, general?' said Mr. Wyndham, with deep earnestness, hardly able to speak for emotion.

'I will, Wyndham, as if they were my own.'

'Thank you. God bless you! I have no fear of their being left without a friend while you are preserved: and then there is One still who I know will never leave them— never forsake them,' rejoined the dying man. 'And you, gentlemen,' he added, addressing Sir Henry Smith and Mr. West, 'I am thankful to you for your attention and services, and believe you have done all that could be done to prolong my life. But it's all in vain. He, before whom the power and skill of man are as nothing, is against you, and has made all your efforts ineffectual. His will be done!'

'Don't you think we might manage to get Mr. Wyndham carried upstairs to his bed, Dr. Smith?' asked General Fielden, after another short, solemn pause, in which there was nothing heard but breathing and suppressed sobs of Blanche Wyndham and her mother.

'I am almost afraid it would be too much for him. He seems pretty free from pain at present, and the least motion, or exertion on his part, might bring it on again, as well as increase the internal hemorrhage, which appears to be rather less than it was.'

'No, don't move me. I am quite comfortable where I am,' said Mr. Wyndham, opening his eyes, after having lain a few minutes with them shut, as if asleep, during which his wife and daughter had stood bending over him, watching his calm quiet breathing with absorbing interest. There was a gentle smile of the deepest affection upon his face as he met their looks of sorrowful tenderness fixed intently upon his countenance.

'Do not be so distressed, my beloved ones,' he said in a low earnest voice; 'God will not leave you without comfort. And it's a consolation to me that He has not taken me away before I have seen the cruel error I was committing in trying to force you, my dear child, to marry one so unworthy of you, and been able to undo that injustice to you before it was too late. God forgive me for my folly!'

'Oh, dear papa! Do not think of that now. If you would only recover and live, I would do anything to please you—anything to make you happy,' said Blanche, earnestly.

'So you always have done, my dear child; may God bless you!' said the father, faintly smiling as he spoke.

At this moment there was a slight tap at the door, and, on General Fielden softly opening it, he found Eliza Fleming, who, almost as much distressed as her mistress herself, had come to say that Mr. Anstruther had called to hear how her master was, which he immediately communicated to Mrs. Wyndham, who, after a few moments' consultation with the general and the doctor, said in a quiet tone to her husband:

'Mr. Anstruther has called to inquire

how you are, dear. Would you like to see him?'

'Yes, dear, I should very much,' he replied, with a glad smile.

Mr. Anstruther was immediately admitted.

'Oh, Mrs. Wyndham! I am so shocked and sorry to hear of this great trial of yours, and the dangerous state of your husband. But I sincerely hope he is not so ill as your servant has informed me,' said the clergyman in a low earnest voice, shaking her warmly by the hand as she met him at the door of the room, and giving a slight start as he saw the serious looks of General Fielden and the doctors, and the pale face of Mrs. Wyndham.

'I fear, Mr. Anstruther, what the servant has told you is only too true. My poor dear husband is—is dying,' she replied with a convulsive sob, as she led him forward to her husband, who, as the clergyman approached, feebly held out his hand, with a faint smile of welcome, which Mr. Anstruther took hold of and pressed gently, but affectionately, apparently too much overcome by his feeling to be able, for a few moments, to speak.

'This is very kind of you, Mr. Anstruther; I am so glad you have come. I had just been wishing that you were here,' said the invalid, in a calm, kindly voice.

'Oh, Mr. Wyndham, I did not expect to find you thus when I came in. So suddenly cut down,' said the clergyman.

'Ay, it is sudden, Mr. Anstruther. But I hope God will have mercy upon me,' returned Mr. Wyndham humbly, but hopefully.

'I should like to hear once more the proclamation of His mercy to guilty sinners, and to partake of the memorials of His death, and the tokens of man's salvation, before I take my departure from this world, to stand before Him in His kingdom,' he added with calm earnest fervour, while the clergyman immediately prepared to comply with his request.

We will now drop the curtain on this sad scene. We dare not intrude upon the holy service of religion in the last moments of the dying man, whose soul was cheered and refreshed by the blessed words he heard, and strengthened and comforted by the heavenly support he received from the holy ordinance of which he was permitted to partake.

Mr. Anstruther performed his duties with the earnestness of a man who was fully aware of the awfulness of the moment, and full of faith in the efficacy of Him whose glorious promises he proclaimed, and the sacred memorials of whose death he now administered. Nor did the rest of his hearers fail to receive both comfort and support from his holy office, which all present took part in with the deepest reverence and solemnity.

A few minutes after this, a sharp, shrill shriek arose in the room and rang through the house. It was the agonising cry of Blanche Wyndham as the spirit of her father took its flight up to God, and his inanimate head dropped forward on his bosom, and his eyes became fixed and expressionless, never more to look upon her with the fond smile of an affectionate parent, or to return her bright intelligent glance of confidence and love in this world, from which his soul had now departed.

Mrs. Wyndham was scarcely less overcome than her daughter, but the piercing shriek of the latter, as she sunk down in a swoon, fortunately caught by General Fielden before she reached the floor, tended in some measure to break the force of her mother's grief, who, with stifled sobs, turned round to her assistance, and strove to restore her to consciousness, which with the help of the doctors, and the ready aid of Eliza Fleming and a couple of the general's female servants, was soon accomplished, but not before they had carried her out of the room and laid her down upon a couch in the drawing-room.

CHAPTER XV.

LITTLE dreaming of the awful change that had just taken place, William Haverty and his father had just arrived at General Fielden's door to inquire for Mr. Wyndham, when the startling shriek of Blanche rang through the house and fell upon their ears. For the moment they stood appalled at the awful truth which it instantly stamped upon their minds; and they scarcely dared to ring the bell for admittance. The footman, however, who was in the hall, hearing them outside, opened the door and told them that Mr. Wyndham was dead!

'I feared so, from that cry we just heard,' said the colonel, solemnly.

'Yes, that was the poor young lady. Oh, it was such a shriek! It went through my heart like a knife!' said the footman, with a slight tremor in his honest voice; while William Haverty could scarcely stand for agitation, and dared not trust his voice to speak.

'She is not ill, I hope, is she?' inquired the colonel, anxiously.

'No; I believe she has only fainted. But, oh, that cry of hers was awful to hear,' said the footman, earnestly.

Just at this moment Blanche Wyndham was being brought across the hall into the drawing-room, and General Fielden, who was opening the door for those carrying her, caught sight of his old friend and his son, and immediately advanced to meet them.

'Oh, colonel, poor Wyndham is gone!' said he, with much emotion.

'I had no idea he was in such immediate danger,' replied the colonel, not less agitated.

'Neither had I when I saw you this morning. But it's all over now. Poor Wyndham!'

'Ay, poor Wyndham!' repeated the colonel, solemnly. 'I hope God has had mercy on his soul!'

'I hope, and trust—yea, I believe He has,' said General Fielden, with calm confidence, adding, after a moment's pause: 'Do you know, I almost envy him. He died so calmly, hopefully and peacefully !'

'God Almighty be praised !' exclaimed Colonel Haverty, with fervent earnestness; 'and how is dear Mrs. Wyndham? and Blanche? I hope God will support them in their affliction. We heard the piercing shriek of poor Blanche as we came to the door, and suspected what it was.'

'Oh, colonel, such a shriek as I hope I shall never hear again ! It seemed to chill my very life's blood with horror. It was the most wildly painful cry I ever heard. Fortunately I was close to her, and caught her as she was falling in a swoon. But I hope she will soon recover.'

'I hope she is not in danger, general,' said William Haverty, trembling with agitation.

'I don't think she is, and we have Sir Henry Smith, from Westdon, as well as Mr. West, still here. I believe they do not apprehend any danger. Would you like to see Mrs. Wyndham?'

'Can I be of any service to her, do you think?' asked the colonel, in reply.

'I don't know. But perhaps she might like to see you. Step in while I let her know you are here,' said the general, showing them into a small breakfast-room, and then went to acquaint her of their call. Presently he returned with Mrs. Wyndham, who was too much overcome with grief to speak for some minutes.

'My dear Mrs. Wyndham!' said Colonel Haverty, as he held out his solitary left hand and shook hers heartily and sympathisingly with it; 'I cannot express to you how much we are shocked and grieved at this awfully sudden death of dear Mr. Wyndham! or how deeply we feel for and sympathise with you and your daughter.'

'Oh, colonel!' said Mrs. Wyndham, with a deep, choking sigh; 'it is an awful trial to us! but I hope God will help us to bear it; for I feel as if, without His support, I should sink under it.'

'May He grant you the strength and consolation you need!' returned the colonel, fervently. 'I am so sorry I did not know that poor Wyndham was so ill, that I might have seen him once more before he died.'

'We had no idea, when William left us this morning, that he was in any immediate danger,' said Mrs. Wyndham, sobbing violently; nor could either the colonel or the general restrain their own emotions, while

William was even more overcome than they, and stood, with his face toward the window, vainly trying to force back the large tears which rose to his eyes, and to stifle the swelling agitation of his heart.

'Mrs. Wyndham,' at length said the general, 'we must endeavour to bear His judgments patiently. It is a great consolation to think that your husband died so calmly and hopefully. I have no doubt whatever but what is a great loss and affliction to all of us, and especially to you and your daughter, has been a great and eternal gain of peace and happiness to him. I have no doubt but he is already in the enjoyment of that felicity in the presence of his Redeemer, which we all look forward to and hope for. Let us not be selfish then, and murmur that he has been taken from us, and translated from a world of sorrow, pain and trial, to one of endless joy, purity, and blessedness.'

There was a deep, fervent earnestness in his voice and manner as he said this, which was not without effect upon Mrs. Wyndham, who, after a short silence, replied with emotion:

'Yes, general, it is a great comfort to me to feel that what is a trial to us, is a blessed happiness to him; and I hope God will give me patience to bear my affliction without repining at His dispensations—for it is hard, very hard! to be so suddenly deprived of so good and tender a husband.'

'As an old friend of both yours and your husband, Mrs. Wyndham,' said the colonel, 'I hope you will allow me and 'my son to offer our assistance to you in any way you may require it. General Fielden, I know, will only be too happy to do everything in his power to serve you; but if there should be anything that we can do to assist you, I hope you will not hesitate to ask us.'

'Thank you. I know your kindliness of nature too well to scruple about doing so, should I require it; and I have had too good a proof of your son's readiness to serve us already to need any further assurance of his willingness. Should I find it requisite to employ the good offices of either, I will not fail to let you know. Oh, I feel I can never be too grateful to you, William,' she added, addressing him as he turned round from the window, 'for what you have already done for us. Oh, colonel, but for him, I might have now had to mourn not only the loss of my dear husband, but the fearful death of my daughter also.'

'Mrs. Wyndham,' said William with emotion, 'it is a great consolation and happiness to me to know that I have been in any way instrumental in lessening your affliction, by saving Blanche from the dreadful fate with which she was threatened. My only regret and sorrow is the untimely death of Mr. Wyndham.'

'I hope all your husband's papers and valuable documents were saved from the fire, Mrs. Wyndham?' remarked Colonel Haverty.

'Yes, I believe they were. General Fielden kindly looked after them, and brought them to his house last night.'

'I am so glad of that. It is very fortunate.'

'It is indeed,' replied the general. 'I believe I am one of Mr. Wyndham's executors; the papers will be of most essential service to us. The will, I suppose, will be among them,' he added, turning to Mrs. Wyndham.

'I suppose it is, but perhaps you will kindly look them over and see, for I cannot touch them.'

'Do not, my dear Mrs. Wyndham, trouble yourself about anything. I will do everything necessary to be done; and if I should want any advice about anything, I'll consult our friend here.'

'And I shall only be too glad if I can be of the slightest assistance or service,' returned the colonel.

'Miss Blanche would like to see you, please, ma'am,' said Eliza Fleming, entering the room, after knocking gently at the door and being desired to come in.

'She is not ill again, I hope?' said Mrs. Wyndham, with an anxious look.

'No, ma'am; only she's uneasy, I think, at not seeing you.'

'Will you go in and see my daughter, colonel?— Come, William, it will perhaps cheer her up to see you and your father,' said Mrs. Wyndham, rising and leading the way into the room where Blanche was, almost sinking down with agitation as she passed the door of the room where her husband still lay.

CHAPTER XVI.

GENERAL FIELDEN was unable to find Mr. Wyndham's will among the rest of his papers, and without that he knew not how to act. That Mr. Wyndham had made one he felt certain, for it was only a few weeks before that he had asked him to become one of his executors and trustees; and Mrs. Wyndham herself had seen him reading it over only a few days before the fire.

It never, however, struck the general that the paper he and William Haverty had seen Bilson pick up on the morning after the fire might be it. He had searched among the ruins of the house, and inquired at Mr. Wyndham's solicitor's, in Westdon, in vain. No tidings of the will could be found. The solicitor told him he had made one, and that he and Mrs. Wyndham were the executors, and that Mr. Wyndham had had it in his own possession before his death. This only increased the general's anxiety to find it, and, a few days after Mr. Wyndham's funeral, with the concurrent advice of the widow and Colonel Haverty, whom they consulted in everything connected with the matter, a few handbills were printed, and an advertisement published in the local papers, offering a reward of one hundred pounds to anyone who could produce the will. But no will was forthcoming. The fear which they had from the first entertained, that it had been consumed in the fire, became in consequence more strongly impressed upon the minds of both Mrs. Wyndham and General Fielden, and they now almost began to despair of ever recovering it.

In the meantime, the restored confidence and renewed happiness between Blanche Wyndham and William Haverty—except so far as it was saddened by recent events and sorrowful recollections—flowed on uninterrupted. Blanche, with the elasticity of a youthful mind and naturally buoyant spirit, soon regained much of her cheerfulness and healthful appearance. And she was the more anxious to do this for the sake of her mother, whose grief for the loss of her husband seemed rather to increase than diminish with time. Nor did her old friends fail in doing their best to cheer her in her sorrow. The good old Mrs. Haverty forgot the slight shyness that had lately been exhibited by the Wyndhams, attended her like a sister, and strove to console and comfort her with all the earnestness of long-tried, sincere friendship and affection. The whole neighbourhood was moved with sympathy for her sufferings and affliction. Even the Ingrams and the Days had both sent several times to inquire for her and her daughter, and would have called themselves, but for the reply to a message they had sent to that effect, that Mrs. Wyndham was not able to see any visitors at present.

Mr. James Murray had also called once or twice, and, as if nothing whatever had occurred to interrupt his previous position with respect to Blanche, inquired about the health of herself and Mrs. Wyndham, but of course had not been asked into the house; and he had taken care neither to appear surprised at this, nor to look as if he had expected to see them yet. General Fielden, too, had always avoided meeting him, for two reasons, the first of which was his own unwillingness to have any intercourse with a man for whom he entertained so complete a contempt, and yet that sort of reluctance one feels to treat with disrespect a man with whom he had been in the habit of meeting, and more or less associating with, for years, both in the discharge of public duties and in private life; and his second was his determination to allow him no chance or opportunity of seeing Blanche Wyndham.

One day about this time, as General Fielden was sitting by himself in his own small room, he took up his London newspaper, which had just been brought in by the servant, and the first thing he saw was the ominous words :

'Indian News.—Telegram from Marseilles.— Mutiny of the Bengal Army, and reported Massacre of Europeans!'

For some moments he could read no more. The paper almost dropped from his hands, and he sat in abstracted agitation, gazing upon those terrible words.

He had not, however, sat long when Colonel Haverty, who always called once a day, and sometimes twice, to inquire for Mrs. Wyndham and Blanche, was announced by the servant, and shown into the room. Sometimes he called without coming in; but the general had desired his servant to say he wished to see him if he called.

'How do you do, colonel? I am so glad you have come in, as I wished to see you. I have just received a very important piece of intelligence, which I was anxious to communicate to you,' said the general, as he shook the colonel by the hand.

'You've found where the will is, I hope?'

'No; I am sorry to say I have not. But just look at that!' handing him the newspaper.

'"Mutiny of the Bengal Army!—Massacre of Europeans!"' gasped the colonel, in horrified surprise, repeating the words half to himself. 'Good God! What can this mean?'

'That those infernal Sepoys, that we have been pampering for years, and some of their treacherous chiefs that we have been making a fuss about and treating with so much sentimental folly, have revolted against our authority, and slaughtered our countrymen, I suppose—and women too, I fear, from what this paper says,' rejoined General Fielden, bitterly, again glancing at the telegram.

'Yes,' here it is,' he continued, running his eye over the following few important lines:

'We have just received, *via* Marseilles, intelligence of a great mutiny in the Native Bengal Army, and frightful massacre of European officers, women, and children at Cawnpore, Delhi, and Lucknow. Government, we understand, have received a telegraphic despatch announcing this appalling event, and have already issued orders for the immediate sending out more troops. Full particulars will be given in a day or two.'

'Well, Haverty, what do you think of that?' said his friend, laying down the paper with a serious look.

'Think! Why, I don't know what to think. I am afraid to think!'

'So am I. It will be an awful affair, I fear.'

'I fear so too.'

'I suppose we shall have to send out large reinforcements immediately if we don't want to lose the country altogether. I am glad to see that the Government have already acted with such promptness in this respect.'

'I only hope it won't be too late by the time the fresh troops reach there. I wonder if my son's regiment will be sent out?'

'It is very probable, I think. Will your son accompany his regiment if it goes?'

'I am afraid he will; though he is hardly strong enough, yet, to go to India,' replied the colonel.

'It will be hard work; and we shall want all the force we can spare to suppress this revolt, which I have long feared would take place one of these days.'

'I fear it will be dreadful work, and will require better men than we appear to have there at present to suppress it.'

'And yet we have some first-rate men there,' said the general, though they are, generally, in the wrong place I fear. But I dare say the Government will send out someone else, though I hardly know who we have worth sending, unless it is your old friend, Sir Colin Campbell; and, at his age, perhaps he might not feel disposed to go.'

'He's the only man, I believe, that we have worth sending out; and I hope the Government will send him. I've no doubt but he'll go, if he feels that by doing so he would really be serving his country,' said the colonel.

'I hope he will. He is the only man we have capable of commanding a great army.

I suppose, if he goes, your son will accompany him?'

'I've no doubt of it. William has gone into the town to-day, and I shouldn't wonder but he may hear something further there.'

'Perhaps he may. I should like to hear if he does.'

'I dare say you'll see him. But how are the ladies?'

'I think Mrs. Wyndham is beginning to look a little more cheerful. Only she is very uneasy about the will. I fear it has been burned. Nearly the whole of the ruins have now been examined, but not a vestige of it has been seen.'

'It is very unfortunate. If anyone had found it, I should have thought the hundred pounds reward you have offered would have made them bring it forward. But you must rest in hope. Blanche, I hope, is well?'

'Yes, she is very well, only very anxious about her mother. I suppose William will call in the evening to see them, after he returns from Westdon.'

'I dare say he will, though it may not be till late; he has several things to do there, which will take him some little time. He told us not to wait dinner if he was not home at our usual hour. Where are the ladies ?'

'Upstairs, I believe. Shall I let them know you are here ?'

'No ; as they are not in the way I will not disturb them. You'll let them know I called to inquire for them, and left my own and my wife's kindest regards.'

'I will. Good-bye. I hope William will call in the evening.'

" I have no doubt he will, especially if he hears anything more than we have seen about this mutiny. Good-bye,' rejoined the colonel, returning his friendly clasp as he left the room and took his way homeward, excited and agitated at the news he had just heard.

He had not, however, gone many yards when he was met by Patrick O'Brien, who had come in search of him.

' Well, Patrick,' said the colonel, as that gallant Hibernian drew up before him, with his usual military salute, ' anything the matter that you're come to seek me ?'

' No, yer honor ; unless it's a big dispatch just come from the railway station, directed to his honor the captain, with a dail o' radin' outside, an' immediate printed in big red letters on the top o' the same,' replied Patrick.

'Indeed! For my son,' said the colonel. 'About this Indian Mutiny, I shouldn't wonder,' he added, half to himself.

'About what did yer honor plaise to say?' inquired Patrick, whose ears as well as his eyes were always on the alert.

'I've just heard, from General Fielden, that a mutiny has broken out in the native Bengal army, Patrick, and that there has been a great massacre of Europeans by the Sepoys.'

'Och, the murtherin' villains! I beg yer honor's pardon,' said Patrick, checking himself; 'but sure an' thim Saypoys haven't been afther turnin' agin' our quain and counthry, an' killin' an' murtherin' our counthrymen?'

'I'm afraid they have, though,' replied the colonel, as he walked on, followed by Patrick.

'Thin, by the holy St. Pathrick! only let Pathrick O'Brien get among thim, an' if he don't taich thim something to improve their manners—the haithen spalpeens!—may the counthry o' his birth niver own him as a son again;' he muttered to himself, as he fell behind the colonel, and followed him along the road leading to the village.

When he reached home, Colonel Haverty found his wife in a good deal of uneasy anxiety about the telegraphic despatch.

'I am so alarmed about this dreadful-looking thing,' said she. 'What can it be? I did not like to open it, or I would have done so to relieve my mind.'

'I think I can tell what it is about, my dear,' replied her husband, affectionately. 'I have just seen a London newspaper at General Fielden's, which states that a great mutiny has broken out in the Bengal native army, which has risen against its European officers and massacred them, and a large number of men, women, and children besides.'

'Oh, I hope it isn't true!' exclaimed Mrs. Haverty, earnestly, with a shudder.

'I fear there is little ground to support such a hope, my dear. It is also stated in the paper that the Government have already issued orders for the speedy sending out of reinforcements from this country.'

'Oh, I hope our dear boy is not going to be sent out to India!' exclaimed the wife, with alarmed anxiety.

'Well, I dare say he doesn't need to go unless he likes; but if his regiment goes, and his services are required, I don't think he would be inclined to shrink from his duty and stay at home, my dear. Nor do I think that you, any more than myself, however much we should prefer the happiness of his being with us, and tremble for his safety if he went, would wish him to do so.'

'No, my dear; I should never wish him to do anything unworthy of his own honour or of your son.'

'Or your own either, my darling!' said her husband proudly, interrupting his wife.

'Well, perhaps of mine too,' said she, with a quiet smile. 'But it is very hard if we have to part with him again so soon! And when I think of his terrible sufferings and dangers in that dreadful Crimea, it makes my very heart quake with fear and anxiety!'

'Ay, but I hope our Government had a lesson there that will be useful to them now. But it's no use frightening ourselves till we know what this really is. It may, after all, be about something else,' said her husband, evidently wishing that it might.

Shortly after their son returned from Westdon. He had heard there of the mutiny, and hastened back to acquaint his father and mother of it.

'Oh, I have heard such important news!' he exclaimed as he entered the room, a good deal excited, where his father and mother were sitting. 'The native Bengal army has mutinied, killed the officers, and massacred a great number of European women, and even children! The whole of Westdon is filled with excitement about it.'

'I have just come from General Fielden's, and saw the account in his London paper,' replied his father, with a concerned look. 'But here is a telegraphic message for you, which came up from the railway station a short time ago,' he added, handing him the telegram as he spoke.

'For me!' said the son, with a look of surprise, hastily opening the envelope, and running his eye over the few words it contained; his father and mother anxiously watching his face as he did so.

'A message from the Horse Guards, requesting me, if able for service, to join my regiment, which has been ordered to prepare for going to India; and will sail from Sheerness in a fortnight at furthest,' said he, with constrained composure, looking at his parents.

'Oh, William!' exclaimed his mother, earnestly, with much agitation; 'don't go! You are not well enough to go yet.'

'My dear mother, I'm afraid I must go. I am quite strong enough again for service, and I cannot shirk from my duty. Although I shall feel it very hard to leave you and my father again,' said the son, with emotion.

'God Almighty knows, William, how unwilling I am, as well as your dear mother, for you to leave us again, especially at our age; but I cannot attempt to dissuade you from going where your duty to your queen and country, and your own honour alike, call you. If this revolt is so general, as I fear it is, it will require all the force we can send to crush it—and crushed it must be!' exclaimed the gallant old soldier, stamping his foot with excitement; 'and if the Sepoys have been guilty of the cruelties—which I too much fear is only too true also—if they have massacred our country-women, the loving wives and lovely daughters of our officers and soldiers, and sacrificed their innocent, helpless children, by the God that made me I would go myself, old as I am, maimed as I am, I would go myself, if the Government would let me, and execute justice on the fiendish perpetrators of such horrible butchery!'

As the colonel said this his eyes flashed from beneath his large, gray eyebrows, his features worked with impassioned excitement, and his solitary left arm and hand were raised above his white head, with an energy and intense earnestness of look, which showed that the fiery spirit of his country, and the ardent courage of his youth, was still as strong and ready to meet the enemies of old England, and support the cause of justice and humanity, as they were five-and-forty years before, when he led on his gallant men in the glorious struggles of Vittoria and Salamanca, and stormed the terrible battlements of Badajos and Ciudad Rodrigo: a spirit and a courage which had neither been subdued by old age, nor lessened by forty years' rest from active service.

'But I am too old and mutilated now to fight for the honour of our beloved queen and country, our wives and children,' he added, with a half sad, kindly glance at his wife, whose calm, deep attachment to her husband was only partially displayed in the quiet, gentle smile of admiration and sympathy with which she met his looks and heard his words.

'Ay, my dear, you can only stay at home

and comfort your poor old wife, when our boy is away fighting for us.'

'And the pleasantest of all my duties is this last,' replied her husband, with affection. 'When are you required to give an answer, William?' he asked, turning to his son.

'I see it says within two days, and, I suppose, I shall have to leave here for head quarters as soon as I can,' he replied slowly, and half sadly, thinking of Blanche Wyndham.

'Ay, and it will be long before we see you again, if ever we do!' said his mother, sorrowfully.

'Oh, perhaps not, mother,' he replied, with cheerful affection. 'If we are successful in suppressing the mutiny, I daresay we shall be sent home again before long.'

'But oh, William! if you fall into the hands of those dreadful Sepoys, whatever shall I do?' asked his mother, with emotion.

'Oh, no fear of that. If we have a good commander, I have little fear of them.'

'I hope Sir Colin Campbell will be sent out with you as commander-in-chief,' said his father.

'I hope so too; and, if he is, I shall have no anxiety as to the result. I should like very much to know,' he added, after a moment's pause.

'So should I,' returned the colonel. 'But perhaps you will in a day or two.'

'Most likely. To-morrow I must write to say I intend going with the regiment, and wait orders when to join it.'

'I suppose you'll call at General Fielden's this evening, and let him and the Wyndhams know about this. I told him you would most likely do so, if you heard anything further about the mutiny.'

'Yes, I shall walk over after dinner. How were Mrs. Wyndham and Blanche?'

'I didn't see them. They were upstairs and I would not let them be disturbed; but he told me he thought Mrs. Wyndham was looking a little more cheerful and Blanche was well.'

'What will poor Blanche say to your going away again, William?' inquired his mother, anxiously. 'It will be bad news for her, I'm afraid.'

'Ay, poor girl, I'm afraid it will,' rejoined the colonel, kindly.

'You must cheer her up when I'm gone, mother,' said the son with a forced smile, unwilling to show how much he felt upon this point. 'I suppose they have had no tidings of the will yet,' he added changing the subject.

'None whatever. I fear it must have been destroyed in the fire,' returned his father.

'I fear it too. I suppose Mrs. Wyndham and Blanche will remain with the general till their own house is rebuilt. I see they are getting on with it only slowly.'

'Yes, tradespeople in Westdon don't get on with their work very rapidly. I believe Mrs. Wyndham and her daughter will remain with the general till their house is ready. He will not hear of their going anywhere else.'

'It's very kind of him; but nothing more than I should have expected from his generous disposition. But it is very unfortunate the will can't be found, as he doesn't know how to act.'

'Yes, it is. We shall see if this hundred pounds reward produces any effect,' said the colonel.

'I sincerely hope it may,' rejoined the son, little dreaming of the effect it might have against himself, if the will was found.

CHAPTER XVII.

'WELL, William, have you heard anything more about this terrible mutiny?' asked General Fielden as the former entered the room in the evening where he and Mrs. Wyndham and Blanche were sitting.

'Nothing more than what was in the paper you showed my father this morning, except that I have received this,' he replied, handing the paper containing the telegram to the general, who exclaimed as he glanced at it:

'What! a telegram message?'

'Yes, read it,' said William quietly.

'Mrs. Wyndham and Blanche gave a look of surprise, and the latter of some alarm, as they heard these words.

'There is nothing wrong, I hope, William,' said the former, as she saw the instant look of the general as he read the message.

'No, Mrs. Wyndham; it is only a message from the Horse-Guards,' he replied with apparent composure.

'The Horse-Guards, William? What is it about?' inquired Blanche with an alarmed look, which it was both gratifying and painful for him to witness. It was gratifying to see how much she felt interested in whatever related to or affected him; and painful on account of the uneasiness it gave her.

'I am glad to see that the home government are going to act with such promptitude and despatch in sending out fresh troops; though I am sorry you are ordered off so suddenly, William,' said General Fielden, kindly, as he folded up the paper and handed it back to him.

'Oh! I hope you are not going to be sent out to India among those horrid Sepoys, William?' said Mrs. Wyndham, earnestly.

'I am afraid I am though, Mrs. Wyndham,' he replied calmly, at the same moment meeting the alarmed glance of Blanche, who, changing colour, eagerly, and almost entreatingly, exclaimed:

'Oh William! do not go! Mamma, tell him he must not go!'

'I am afraid, my dear, if he won't be dissuaded by you, he will hardly be by me,' replied Mrs. Wyndham, with a grave but kindly look at William, and with an affectionate glance at the earnest face of her daughter. 'But must you really go, William?' she inquired.

'I fear I must,' he replied sadly.

'What do your father and mother say to it?' asked the general.

'They are both very unwilling for me to leave them; but, at the same time, see that I cannot honourably refuse to go, even if I were inclined.'

'Which you are not, I trust.'

'No. It grieves me more than I have words to express, to think I must again, and so soon, leave those so dear to me,' he said with a choking sensation in his throat, 'but, I would not, if I could, shirk my duty to my country at a time when my services are required by it.'

'Spoken like a true Haverty!' exclaimed the general heartily. 'And now, my dear Mrs. Wyndham and Blanche, you must not try to dissuade him from the performance of his sacred duties as a soldier. You would not, I am sure, long continue to respect him if he allowed any objects of his own, however dear to his heart—and I know there are objects very dear to his heart for which he would fain stay at home—to prevent him from fulfilling his duty to his Queen and country: at a time, too, when not only the lives of tens of thousands of our fellow-countrymen and country-women are at stake, but the very existence of our Indian Empire itself is imperilled by the mutiny of the native army! And, if this is true about the massacre of Europeans, of the inhuman slaughter—ay! and perhaps worse than that, even, of women and poor helpless little children! it ought to make him rise above his own personal feelings, and urge him on to take vengeance, just and righteous vengeance! on the perpetrators of such fiendish cruelties.'

'Oh, but I hope it is not true that they have massacred the women and children,' said Mrs. Wyndham compassionately.

'I wish I could believe they had not,' said General Fielden; 'but I fear there is little ground for such hope. I know the character of those wretches too well, to think they would hesitate at the perpetration of any villany, if they once had the chance. But we shall have full particulars in a day or two, I dare say. Then you have really decided upon going with your regiment?' he added, addressing William.

'Yes, I feel, like you, that, while it would be a dishonour to me, at any time, it would be doubly so at the present, to shrink from my duty as a soldier, however reluctant I am to leave my parents, and—and one—who is dearer to me than—my own life,' said William almost unable to speak from emotion.

'Well, keep a good heart, my dear boy,' said the general, who was evidently much moved, but strove to conceal it; ' and I shall take care of them all—and myself too, if you like—till you come home again,' he added with a cheerful smile.

'Thank you, general, I have too much knowledge of your goodness, as well as confidence in it, to doubt that,' returned William gratefully, 'and as for taking care of yourself I cannot use a stronger argument to induce you to do so, than by reminding you of the importance of the trust you have taken upon you, and which I shall hope for a good account of when I return,' he added with a fond smile.

'Shall you be required to leave soon?' asked Mrs. Wyndham, for Blanche seemed afraid to trust herself to speak.

'The regiment is ordered to sail for Sheerness within a fortnight,' he replied.

'Within a fortnight!' exclaimed Blanche, turning pale at the thought. 'How cruel to force you away so suddenly.'

'I am afraid it is because circumstances require it, my dear Blanche,' rejoined General Fielden kindly.

'It is very short notice, certainly,' remarked Mrs. Wyndham. 'But come, Blanche,' she added with the instinct of a true woman, 'we must not try to make William low-spirited. We ought rather to conceal our regrets at parting with him for a time, and endeavour to cheer him up in the prospect of his so soon leaving, and the dangers which are before him. I hope God will protect him, and bring him home again in safety and honour.'

'Amen! Mrs. Wyndham,' said the general cheeringly. 'I suppose you take your man, Patrick, with you,' he added, addressing William.

'Yes, if he wishes to go; and I don't think he is likely not to wish that.'

'I hope he will go with you,' said Mrs. Wyndham. 'Oh, William! I cannot tell you how much indebted I feel to him for what he did for my poor husband.'

'I only wish his endeavours to save him had not met with the unfortunate accident which befel them at last,' he replied sympathisingly.

'But that was not his fault, poor fellow; and it was very lucky he escaped so well as he did when my poor husband fell upon him.'

'Oh, he has the lives of a dozen people in him, I think,' returned the captain, with a grave smile. 'He never comes to any harm, and is always ready for every emergency, and prepared for every danger.'

'You will come here in the morning, or send, and let us know if you learn anything further about this mutiny, or your own going,' said General Fielden, as William rose to go, who longed for a few minutes' conversation with Blanche, but could find no opportunity.

Delicacy for herself, and consideration for her grief, had hitherto induced him to avoid pressing his suit since the death of her father; but now that the immediate prospect of a long separation was again before him, he found it impossible to resist any longer his strong desire to pour into her ear the full deep passion of his heart. He was determined, therefore, to seek an early opportunity of doing so, and of receiving from her own lips the assurance of her love, to support him in his future dangers and struggles on the far-off burning sands of India.

'Yes, I shall call after breakfast, and let you know whether I have any news or not,' he replied, as he wished them good-evening, and reluctantly left the presence of Blanche Wyndham.

CHAPTER XVIII.

THE same electric agent which had brought the startling intelligence of the Indian Mutiny to London, two days before, had also flashed it through every part of the United Kingdom. The whole nation stood aghast with horrified amazement at the appalling description of the tortures and casualties which had been inflicted upon delicate and beautiful women and children by the fiendish Asiatics.

Throughout the whole of the land there was a loud and general wail of grief, lamentation, and sympathy for the unhappy victims of this unparalleled treachery. But the wails of grief and lamentation were speedily drowned in a universal shout and cry for vengeance on the perpetrators of this inhuman butchery. Never were the fiercer energies of a nation more stirred than were those of Great Britain when she heard the fearful accounts of the tortures and sufferings which had been inflicted on the wives, daughters, and helpless infant children of her brave and gallant soldiers by the treacherous Sepoys.

Men and women, young and old, all joined in the tremendous cry for vengeance—speedy, implacable, righteous vengeance! Justice, policy, and humanity alike demanded it. The power of the country had been defied by her own pampered, traitorous subjects; human nature had been outraged by the diabolical casualties of those Bengal monsters, and both these called for instant and stern retribution.

Away now with all the mawkish sentimentalism of false humanity, and falser policy, which had so long exercised so pernicious an influence on the dealings of Great Britain with her Indian Empire! No more pampering and flattering of deceitful chiefs and perfidious princes now! No more fastidious delicacy and nourishing of the false systems and obscene immoralities of those wretches, whose unparalleled atrocities had for ever placed them beyond the pale of human sympathy and human mercy! Mercy to them! It would have been a prostitution of the holiest of human sentiments to have talked of mercy to those atrocious villains! —a contumelious injustice to the innocent victims, whose reeking blood, mangled, disfigured bodies cried aloud for retribution from the eternal pits of Cawnpore, Lucknow, and Delhi; and was echoed back and answered—fiercely, ominously answered—by every corner of the British dominions, and heard with sympathy and indignation throughout the whole of the civilised world. Old men shook with the force of their wrath, strong men clenched their teeth with the fierceness of their fury, and delicate women forgot the softness and gentleness of their nature, and joined in the great universal cry for vengeance!

Such were the feelings and passions excited in the hearts of the people—high and low, rich and poor, when the terrific tidings of Bengal treachery and outrage was made known to the country, and lashed the energies of the nation into action, as it were in a moment. Before twenty-four hours had elapsed from the receipt of the first intelligence of the mutiny, orders had been issued for the immediate despatch of nearly ten thousand troops, and preparations made for still larger reinforcements, for the support and assistance of our brave countrymen in India. The whole nation was alive to the terrible emergency. Everyone felt that a crisis had arrived which was to decide the fate of our eastern empire, and which nothing but the most strenuous and speedy efforts of the whole power of the kingdom could enable us to surmount.

The effort was made with a mighty power and rapidity, which not only astonished the whole of Europe, but even ourselves. Thanks to the Russian war, the British army was in a state of efficiency and readiness such as it had not been in for more than thirty years; and no sooner did the news of the Indian rebellion reach the country than several regiments lying at Malta were ordered off to India, and still larger forces sent from England.

A day or two elapsed before Captain Haverty received any further intelligence, except what appeared in the newspapers, respecting his departure. His preparations were speedily made, and, in less than a week, he was ready to start to join his regiment.

As may readily be supposed, in spite of

his devotion to his noble profession, his zeal for the honour of his country and the authority of his beloved queen, William Haverty experienced many sad, sinking sensations of the heart at the thought of parting with his kind, affectionate, and most loved parents. Years, probably, would elapse before he again returned to England : and they might perhaps be long ere that laid in their graves in the quiet churchyard, while he was far, far away amid the arid, hot sands of India, all unconscious of their death, and never more to see them in this world, or listen to their dear voices in counsel or affection.

Such saddening thoughts often and often occurred to him during the few days occupied in making preparations for his departure. Nor were those excited by the near prospect of leaving Blanche Wyndham less painful. Recent events and circumstances had so strengthened and increased his love for her, that he never felt happy but in her society ; and the thought of leaving her, and so soon being so many thousands of miles from her, with no prospect of again seeing her for years, was one which might well cause no small amount of depression and regret to his spirits and heart. But he manfully strove against it, and, to conceal it from others, often looked cheerful and lighthearted, when he was very far from feeling either the one or the other.

But how are we to describe the feelings of Blanche Wyndham, who, in spite of her heroic struggles with her own heart to conceal her emotions and to appear cheerful, felt a deep foreboding of coming evil take hold of her mind and chill her blood the moment his departure was announced to her. Anxiety for herself had less share of her thoughts than fear for him. She pictured to herself the long voyage, weary marches over the burning sands, and beneath the scorching sun of India; the fatal fevers, privations, dangers, and the fearful struggles he would have to sustain against the terrible hordes of fierce, ruthless, savage rebels, whose late atrocities showed too well how little mercy might be expected by those who fell into their blood-stained hands.

And yet, though her chief anxiety was for him, Blanche Wyndham was not without some uneasiness for herself also. Somehow there was a vague feeling of dread in her mind lest James Murray should again, during William's absence, make any attempt to renew his attentions to her, or try to force her into that marriage, which he had before been so nearly successful in attaining, the more so as she had heard from General Fielden that James Murray was still talking among his friends, as if he considered the matter merely postponed for a time, till she and her mother had recovered from their grief for the loss of Mr. Wyndham. This she had, with the noble sacrifice of her sex, kept from William Haverty, unwilling that he should have one thought of uneasiness on her account, when he left, that she could possibly keep to herself; and he had too much confidence in her love to have any fear of her fidelity during his absence.

CHAPTER XIX.

HAVING waited some time after the offer of the hundred pounds for the recovery of Mr. Wyndham's will, in the hope of a still larger sum being made, and not finding any forthcoming, Bilson, at length, after much urging from James Murray, resolved to deliver it up, and claim the reward. But there was a difficulty in doing this that he had not before thought of. How was he to accomplish it without exciting suspicion as to the way he came into possession of the will? Would he not be suspected of having stolen it? He had not forgotten that General Fielden, to whom the will was to be delivered, had seen him on the morning he picked it up at Bilford Hall, and had even ordered him away from the place; and would the colonel not at once come to the conclusion that he had found it there and taken it away, if he took it to him and claimed the reward, especially as he well enough knew that General Fielden entertained anything but a favourable opinion of him.

Bilson therefore resolved to employ an intermediate agent in the matter, even though he should have to give him part of the reward, and for this purpose bethought him of one of the workmen who was employed at the rebuilding of the house, which had lately been commenced on the foundation of the old one. This was a drunken fellow, named Brown, who had already been concerned with him in several poaching and other expeditions of an equally disreputable kind. As rogues are always doubtful of each other, Bilson was rather uneasy about trusting the matter to Brown, in case of his keeping the whole of the money himself.

But as he felt he must trust some one and knew no one who would be so little likely to excite suspicion in General Fielden as one of the men who was working at the house, who might easily say that he had found the will among some of the rubbish when removing it.

Bilson therefore went off one evening and

reached Bilford Hall just as the men were leaving off work, and met Brown, saying that he had been out of the village to see about some potatoes a man had for sale, and proposed going back into the village and have a glass of cider at the Ingram Arms, to which the other was both ready and willing to accede, when, after beating about the bush for some time, he at length told Brown about his having found Mr. Wyndham's will, without saying where he had done so, but that, as General Fielden, to whom it was to be given up, had lately been rather sharp with him about something else, he did not like appearing before him with it, and if he thought he could take in hand its delivery, the hundred pounds reward which were offered for it, he should have ten pounds for his trouble.

'But woon't they suspose me too?' inquired Brown.

'No; yee can easy say yee found it among the rubbish where yee was workin',' replied the other.

'Well, I'll du it. Only yee must guv me moar than ten pound.'

'Why, yee ——, isn't that enough for all yee'll ha to do?' said Bilson, with an oath.

'Noa, it bean't,' said the other, who had discernment enough to see that Bilson had come upon the will in a way that he was afraid to tell General Fielden; 'an' oi tell yee what, if yee doant guv me no more nur that, when yee're to hav' so much to yeersel', oi shan't ha' nothin' to du wi' it.'

'Well, how much more do yee want?' asked Bilson, sulkily.

'Another ten pound, if ha' anything a du wi' it.'

'Why, I've no occasion to give you anything, if I like to go and give it up myself.'

'Well, du it, then,' said Brown, who felt sure he dared not, or he would not have asked him at all.

'Come now, Ted, as I want to put something in yer way, I'll give yee another five if yee like to take the job in hand,' said Bilson, as if about to go away.

'But a precious lot mooure into yer own,' returned Brown, gruffly. 'If yee woan't guv me the twou tens, I woan't ba' nothin' whatsomever to do wi' the job.'

'Well, as I have mentioned it to yee, Ted, I suppose I must let yee have it. But mind, yee're not to say that I gave it to yee, or that —— old general will take it from yee, and give yee nothing at all; and then yee'll not only lose the twenty pound, but I shall all mine as well.'

'Ooa! leave Ted Brown aloane for a crammer about that. If they asks me anythin', oi'll take care on that, oi promise yu.'

'Well, then, you meet me here to-morrow after yee've left off work, an I'll give yee the thing to take along to the general, as if yee had just found it, an' he'll give yee the hundred pound reward.'

'Yee ha'n't a got it now, then?' inquired Brown, with a disappointed look.

'Yes, I have. I always carry it with me, 'cause I've no place to keep it in at home where it would be safe; only it'll be better to leave till to-morrow afore yee take it, I think,' replied Bilson, who still felt some reluctance about entrusting the will to Brown.

'Well, just as yee like; oanly the sooner the job's over the better, oi think. But, come, let's ha' another drop o' cider on the strength on it.'

'Very well,' said Bilson, calling to the landlord to bring in some more of that beverage; 'I'm in no hurry. Besides, I've got a hare-gin or two I want to look at afore

I go hame. Will you go with me?' he said, in a lower tone.

'Oah, oi doan't mind. Only yo must guv me some o' the game if I du.'

'Curse ye, Brown! Yee're always so afeard ye doant get enough,' said the other, impatiently. 'A'nt I agoing to give yee twenty pound to-morrow? An' yee make such a precious row about getting part o' the game to-night. Wait till we see if there is any afore yee say anything about gettin' part on it.'

'Bean't oi agoin' to du some'at for the twenty pound, then? So yee needn't be so —— sharp about that, aeither, Master Bilson,' returned the other, roughly. 'But, as yu say, wait till we see what game there is afore we say anything about the dividin' on it.'

The small parlour, or tap-room, where these two worthies held the above conversation, as well as much more which we have not related, was adjoining the room, and only divided from it by a thin wooden partition open at the top, which the landlord of the house and his own family generally occupied; and as both Bilson and Brown were looked upon with considerable suspicion in the neighbourhood, especially the former, when the landlord saw them come in, he not only resolved to keep a sharp eye upon them, but a sharp ear also ; and, for the latter purpose, had seated himself close to the other side of the partition that he might overhear what they said, more from a feeling of curiosity than that he expected any benefit to arise from it either to himself or anyone else.

But what was his surprise when he heard Bilson tell Brown that he not only had the will, for which a hundred pounds reward was offered, but that, at that very moment, it was in his pocket! And, from his roundabout manner and confused tone, he at the same time felt confident that Bilson had come by it in a way which made him afraid to expose himself to any inquiry on the subject. The moment he heard the will mentioned he was doubly on the alert to catch every word that passed between them ; so that he soon learned the whole scheme which Bilson intended employing to secure the hundred pounds for the restoration of the will, which he ought rather to be punished for having in his possession than rewarded for giving up. The landlord was an old servant of Mr. Wyndham's, and still retained great respect and regard for the family, which had been even greater than usual since the sudden death of his old master, and the trials and sufferings of Mrs. Wyndham and Blanche.

He had, of course, heard of the reward that was offered for the recovery of the will; but how it had got into the hands of Bilson was beyond his comprehension, except that he felt quite sure it must have been by some dishonest means; and, believing this, he thought there would be little harm in trying to prevent that fellow from reaping the advantage he expected by its possession.

As soon, therefore, as he had taken in the second pot of cider to Bilson and Brown, and told his wife to keep a sharp look-out upon them in case they went off without paying, the landlord put on his best coat and hat, hastened off to tell General Fielden what he had just heard, intending to call at Colonel Haverty's on his way and inform him also—for both of whom he entertained great respect, especially as he knew them to have been such old friends of poor Mr. Wyndham's, and that they were so much interested in the recovery of his will.

He had not, however, gone far when he met Patrick O'Brien, with whom he was on terms of considerable intimacy and mutual confidence, for Patrick was one of those light-hearted, sociable fellows, who never failed in speedily making the acquaintance of everyone in the neighbourhood, wherever he was, and their good opinion generally at the same time. He, therefore, at once resolved upon taking Patrick into his confidence, and consulting him upon the best means of not only securing the will, but for preventing Bilson from getting the reward that was offered for it.

END OF VOL. II.

BILLING AND SONS, PRINTERS AND ELECTROTYPERS, GUILDFORD.

www.ingramcontent.com/pod-product-compliance
Lightning Source LLC
Chambersburg PA
CBHW032121230426
43672CB00009B/1820